W9-BRL-007

DATE		
OCT 29 '82	AUG 20 1997	
MAY 6 '83	OCT 23 1998	
JAN 3 '88	DEC 28 198	
NOV 28 1987		
FEB 02 1988		
JUN 1 1989		
FEB 06 '91		
JUL 29 '91		
FEB 12 '92		
JUN 29 1993		
APR 08 1996		
OCT 08 1996		

TWAYNE'S WORLD LEADERS SERIES

EDITOR OF THIS VOLUME
Samuel Smith, Ph.D.

Plato

TWLS 66

Plato

PLATO

By WILLIAM S. SAHAKIAN

Suffolk University

MABEL LEWIS SAHAKIAN

Northeastern University

TWAYNE PUBLISHERS

A DIVISION OF G. K. HALL & CO., BOSTON

Library of Congress Cataloging in Publication Data

Sahakian, William S
  Plato.

  (Twayne's world leaders series ; TWLS 66)
  Bibliography: p. 173–79.
  Includes index.
  1. Plato.   I.   Sahakian, Mabel Lewis, joint author.
II.   Title.
B395.S2   184   77-2615
ISBN 0-8057-7690-7

MANUFACTURED IN THE UNITED STATES OF AMERICA

Dedicated to the memory of
Le Roy and Idabel d'Happart

Wonder is the feeling of a philosopher,
and philosophy begins in wonder.
(Plato, *Theaetetus*, 155)

Contents

About the Authors

Dr. Mabel Lewis Sahakian, currently Lecturer in Philosophy at Northeastern University where she has taught since the early 1960's, pursued her Ph.D. in the field of philosophy at Boston University. For almost a decade she has coauthored books with her husband William S. Sahakian. A popular lecturer at civic and church groups, as well as at universities, she has been singled out for a number of honors, including the *World Who's Who of Women; Who's Who of American Women; Contemporary Authors; Two Thousand Women of Achievement;* and *Dictionary of International Biography.* She has been a member of the Boston Authors Club and the American Philosophical Association. She is the coauthor with W. S. Sahakian of *Realms of Philosophy* (1965), *Ideas of the Great Philosophers* (1966), *Rousseau as Educator* (Twayne Publishers, 1974), and *John Locke* (Twayne, 1975). She is included in *Who's Who in America.*

William S. Sahakian undertook his graduate studies at Harvard and Boston Universities, receiving his Ph.D. from the latter institution. He is currently Professor of Philosophy and Psychology at Suffolk University. Dr. Sahakian has contributed to professional journals throughout the world, and his books include *History of Philosophy* (1968); *Ethics: Theories and Problems* (1974); *History of Psychology* (1968); *Psychology of Personality* (rev. ed., 1974); and *Introduction to Psychology of Learning.* He has written articles for the *Encyclopaedia Britannica* and the *International Encyclopedia of Psychiatry, Psychoanalysis, and Psychology.* His past and present professional affiliations include membership in the American Philosophical Association, the American Psychological Association, the New York Academy of Science, and Fellow of the Massachusetts Psychological Association. He has been selected for inclusion in *Who's Who in the World; Who's Who in America; Contemporary Authors; American Men of Science;* and the *International Scholars Directory.*

Preface

To the extent possible, this book has been designed so that the reader may begin with any chapter he prefers. By and large, each chapter is self-contained with definitions pertinent to that specific chapter. The book has also been arranged so that the more difficult chapters follow the less abstruse ones.

Inasmuch as Plato used the dialogue form, putting statements into the mouths of his characters, it is awkward to assert that Plato made this or that statement, when he himself is not one of the characters. He would, therefore, have another person express his viewpoint. Usually this was Socrates, and in the earlier writings, when Plato was under the spell of Socrates, we often attributed the expressed view to Plato's mentor. But as Plato's own ideas matured, we increasingly cite his ideas as Plato's original concepts.

Plato claimed that his philosophy could not be packaged in textbook form, nor would he have considered expressing his philosophy in any but dialogue fashion. In order to retain some of the beauty of these philosophical dialogues, we have quoted liberally where we thought paraphrasing his ideas would do him an injustice.

Because certain Greek terms defy translation, we resorted to using the Greek word together with its commonly translated equivalents. Hopefully, the contextual use will serve as a better determination of the word than our formal definitions. However, since our experience with readers, especially our students, has made us aware that readers of classical Greek seem to become fewer with each passing year, we have transliterated every Greek word. The diacritical marks used are as follows: While *e* (pronounced as in *get*) serves for epsilon, *ē* (pronounced as in *Plato* or *ate*) is eta; *o* (pronounced as in *cod*) is omicron, and *ō* pronounced as in *note*) is omega (while the *o* is short, the *ō* is long); *u* and *y* (pronounced as in the French *tu* or the German *Tür*) are upsilon (transliterated *y* except as the final letter of a diphthong). Other letters used in the Greek words, we trust, will not prove to be a problem, except that gamma is retained as *g* (pronounced as in *get*) even before a velar. Some transliterations, such as that found in the *Encyclopaedia Britannica*, change the *g* to *n* before a velar. This occurs with respect to only one Greek term in this work, the word *necessity*, which is rendered *anagkē* instead of *anankē*. We should hasten to add, however, that *g* (gamma) is pronounced like *ng* before *k* (kappa) or *chi* (pronounced as in the German *ich* or the Scotch *loch*, and transliterated *ch*). Pronunciation of vowels in classical Greek is a virtually insoluble problem. For our purposes as far as the present book is concerned, this lesson should suffice for our instruction in Greek.

WILLIAM S. SAHAKIAN
MABEL LEWIS SAHAKIAN

Wellesley, Massachusetts

Chronology

ca. 850–800 B.C.	Homer's *Iliad* and *Odyssey* open the period of European literature.
776	First Olympic Games.
6th century	Greek philosophy begins.
594	Solon establishes democracy in Athens.
508	Cleisthenes confirms Solon's democracy in Athens.
490	Battle of Marathon.
470	Socrates born.
461–429	Pericles governs Athens (Golden Age of Pericles).
451	Law mandates both parents of a citizen must be Athenian.
431–403	Peloponnesian War.
430–429	Great Plague.
427/8	Plato born.
415	Athenians attempt conquest of Syracuse and Sicily.
409	Plato required to enter military service.
407–399	Plato studies under Socrates; develops his philosophical dialogue with Socrates at age twenty.
406	Socrates opposes the Assembly for acting against the law.
405	Spartans attack Athens.
404	Athens loses war with Sparta.
399	Socrates, convicted of impiety and corrupting the Athenian youth, is sentenced to death; Plato leaves for the house of Euclid in Megara.
395	Plato returns to Athens from Egypt.
387	Plato's first journey to Sicily and southern Italy; treated as a prisoner of war by Dionysius the Elder, he is sold into slavery and shortly thereafter ransomed by Anniceris. Founding of the Academy. Plato begins writing of dialogues.
ca. 367	Plato's second journey to Syracuse and Sicily.

367   Death of Dionysius the Elder.
361   Plato's third journey to Syracuse.
361 or   Plato returns to Athens.
360
347   Death of Plato.
ca. 335 Founding of the Lyceum.
334–   Alexander the Great conquers the Persian Empire.
326
323   Death of Alexander.

CHAPTER 1

Plato's Athens

THE Athens of Plato was a city-state, an independent state with sovereignty vested in its free citizens who owed allegiance, not to Greece as a whole (*Magna Graeca*), but only to their city-state. Consequently, the loss of its independence in the war against Philip of Macedon (shortly after Plato's death in 347 B.C.) profoundly disturbed the Athenians, who had long regarded themselves as superior people and their beloved city as an invincible power. A noted English political scientist, Alfred Zimmern, has remarked upon the deep attachment and loyalty of Athenians to their city-state, a relationship which must be fully appreciated in order to understand the political, social, cultural, and intellectual history of Athens during this period:

The Greek citizen grew up, like the members of some exclusive and favoured institutions, in a different atmosphere. . . . His city was the only city, and her ways the only ways. He loved every rock and spring in the folds of her mountains, every shrine and haunt within the circuit of her walls. . . . When his city brought forth not merely fighters and bards, but architects and sculptors, and all the resources of art reinforced the influence of early association and natural beauty, small wonder that the Greek citizen, as Pericles said, needed but to look at his city to fall in love with her. The Athenian had loved the Acropolis rock while it was still rough and unlevelled, when the sun, peeping over Hymettus, found only ruddy crags and rude Pelasgian blocks to illumine. He loved it tenfold more now, when its marble temples caught the first gleam of the morning or stood out, in the dignity of perfect line, against a flaming sunset over the mountains of the West.[1]

The city, said Aristotle, is not only the highest form of association, but also the one which "embraces all the rest."[2]

13

I *The Agora as the Place of Assembly*

Athenians preferred to conduct their business in the open air instead of indoors. Furthermore, as Plato noted, they liked to "swarm" together. Since they had no means of heating their houses, which were often cold and uncomfortable, they built colonnades (covered walks), where they could at any time stroll and converse. Greek citizens took pride in the colonnades as valuable assets of their city, assets frequently mortgaged as security for public debts.

Agora, the Greek term for a marketplace, originally meant a place of assembly, more specifically a place where the common people, the ordinary citizens in contradistinction from elected or appointed government officials, could assemble for public debates, judicial trials, elections, circulation of news by word of mouth, shopping, and attendance at community celebrations, orations, and political discussions. Public speaking was an outstanding feature of these activities; in fact, the term *agora* was used in some contexts to denote oratorical skill (as in saying, for example, that Demosthenes was the greatest of all men in the agora). Here the space was open to all, even to the children for their games.

II *The State as the Common Interest*

The Greek word *koinon*, which means common interest, shared in common, jointly, or simply common, refers to affairs of the state as a political organization. The common good or commonwealth *(to koinon agathon)* has the same connotation as the Latin term *res publica* used by the Romans to denote the state as a matter of common concern—everybody's business. In Athens politics was in truth an activity to which all free citizens devoted themselves and which they perpetually discussed.

The Greek term *koinōnia*, derived from the same source as *koinon*, means fellowship based upon equal sharing in a common interest. The Christian word *communion* is similar in its connotation when used to mean equal sharing in a common faith expressed outwardly in mutual intercourse and communication. The Athenians, who required no apologetic introductory statements to justify expression of their beliefs, spoke out boldly whatever was in their minds about political issues and leaders. Although the individual's right to privacy in his family affairs was respected, matters of this kind being regarded as personal and not suitable topics for public discussion, politics and politicians were otherwise subjected to unrestricted criticism and free debate. Dictators were condemned less severely for unpopular decisions than for their secretive tactics and refusal to share information with the general public. Candor on the part of a ruler was regarded as essential to government in behalf of the people, to public welfare. This basic purpose of government—to respect and foster the interests of the community—was Aristotle's criterion for discriminating between good and corrupt forms of government. He concluded that reason and justice, enlightenment and concern for the common interest, were permanent factors affecting the worth of a good government irrespective of its contemporary formal structure. For a particular people, time, and place the best government might be a monarchy, for other situations, an aristocracy, or, alternatively, a polity representing the public.

Any such good government, however, would readily become corrupt if the rulers substituted private gain for public welfare as their goal. Thus, according to Aristotle, a good monarchy would become a corrupt tyranny, a good aristocracy would become a corrupt oligarchy, and a good polity (constitutional government) would become a corrupt democracy. Plato and Aristotle condemned democracy as rule by the masses who were motivated, not by reason, but by irrational emotions, and pointed out that it was a democracy which sentenced Socrates to death. Aristotle himself fled Athens, depriving that democracy of a second opportunity to sin against philosophy.

III *The Good Life as a Leisure-Time Activity*

The citizen of ancient Athens cared much more about social intercourse, politics, and academic dialogue than economic gain and never regarded the latter as the proper basis for his main preoccupation or consideration. If he had to choose between the two, he would sacrifice economic advancement for the sake of achievement in his political and social life. In fact, the Greek tongue does not even contain a synonym for commerce or business activity, which is referred to merely as the "absence of leisure" (*ascholia*). An individual's *ascholia* was regarded as a regrettable interference with his participation in worthy leisure-time activities constituting the good life. The word *scholar* was derived from the same term and connotes the opposite of *business*; the Greek *scholē*, meaning leisure, rest, or ease, refers to the serious leisure-time activities conducive to learning, more especially to learned discussion or disputation. Accordingly, Plato and Aristotle considered philosophical inquiry a leisure-time pursuit and accorded to it a priority far above activities of the commercial world. Political or social life, however, was esteemed as being on a par with and, indeed, as being one aspect of philosophy. Plato therefore advocated rule by a philosopher-king, and Aristotle regarded man as a political animal.

Aristotle's "political animal" prized most of all the right to discuss freely any life situations or problems confronting him. Athenians took special pride in permitting individuals the luxury of their idiosyncrasies. Every free citizen was entitled to exercise his preferences with respect to his possessions, actions, and interests. The principle of self-determination, allowing each person to make his own decisions, prevailed—even though in a democratic society public opinion would generally decide legal and political policies and in certain instances control the individual's behavior if, for example, he were misusing his wealth. For the free citizen of Athens, winning honor and a good reputation, not riches, was always the proper motivation and goal in life.

Leisure time was not only highly prized by the Athenian, but indeed well within his grasp, even in the case of an ordinary laborer. A bachelor could earn enough from slightly more than two days of work to make ends meet; and a married man with a wife and two children could just about manage on double that amount of income. Since many of the free citizens were not overburdened by the necessity of earning a living, they could afford to denigrate the value of material success or profitable employment and concentrate their efforts upon the preferred goal of full participation in the public affairs, the political and cultural life, of their city-state. They cherished their leisure-time activities, just as they cherished glory, fame, and service in defense of the nation, and were quite willing to go without material conveniences attainable through burdensome work—those creature comforts whose acquisition motivates our own generation to devote so much energy to moneymaking, often resulting in long hours of labor and excessive nervous tension. In contrast to the modern city dweller, the ancient Greek would never think of wasting precious hours on traveling long distances daily to and from a job. He treasured the opportunity to spend a couple of hours in the afternoon at the public baths and the chance to participate regularly in athletic and cultural activities at the public gymnasium. Referring to the daily habits of the Athenian citizen during the fifth and fourth centuries B.C., H. D. F. Kitto has noted that "the Greek got up as soon as it was light, shook out the blanket in which he had slept, draped it elegantly around himself as a suit, had a beard and no breakfast, and was ready to face the world in five minutes. The afternoon, in fact, was not the middle of his day, but very near the end of it."[3] (Evidently the Athenians, sporting their beards, did not have to waste time on shaving.)

Public service was a paid responsibility; even his attendance at the Assembly entitled the individual to payment for the leisure time he had sacrificed in order to attend. Government officials, members of juries, and others serving the community were similarly indemnified by the state for the time they devoted to the general welfare. This policy, established during the rule of the great statesman Pericles (461–431 B.C.), reflected the truly democratic character of Plato's Athens, the unique experiment in democracy which may well have been the last experiment of its kind, a form of direct, universal participation apparently impossible to permit in modern nations owing to their large size and complexity. In Plato's time individuals could, if they wished, readily participate directly in all aspects of democratic government because the country was small enough for them to traverse within a couple of days even without means of swift transportation.

IV *Family Life*

Animated primarily by political interests and concerns, the free citizen of Athens was a man of the marketplace *(agora)*, a social-minded member of society at large rather than a family man. He depended upon his wife to take care of the home and household affairs, for she was not permitted to join the society of the agora, nor was it safe for her to make the attempt. Respectable women were expected to stay at home in seclusion, a practice reminiscent of the ancient Oriental custom. The selection of a mate was not a matter of voluntary choice but a parental prerogative. Most women married at fifteen, men at thirty years or older.

There was one exception to the rule that Athenian women should be restricted to home duties. An extraordinary group of women,

numbering in the thousands, called the *hetairai* (companions) made
it their business to mingle with the men in the agora for whom they
provided companionship and professional services like those of
Geisha girls in modern Japan. These women were resident aliens
(*metics*) who had been trained to exhibit their expertise in dancing,
music, poetry, sensual attraction, and witty repartee, skills designed
to please and amuse the men in the absence of their wives. In this
way, as the military commander Demosthenes (d. 413 B.C.) pointed
out, Athenian men enjoyed the great advantage of having *hetairai* as
sources of pleasure while their wives bore them legitimate offspring
and served as faithful guardians of the home. But how often the
inhibited wives, restricted to household tasks, must have envied the
hetairai who earned a carefree living by merely giving the men
mutually shared pleasures!

Nevertheless, the women of Athens had considerable influence
over their husbands. The famous Athenian statesman Themistocles
(ca. 527–ca. 460 B.C.) averred that, although he ruled Athens, and
Athens ruled all of Greece, his wife actually ruled him and their
child ruled her.

The resident aliens, the *metics*, from whose ranks the professional
companions of men were recruited, comprised a sizable proportion
of the Athenian population. During the latter part of the fourth
century B.C., the total population of Athens probably averaged
about 300,000 persons if one accepts the estimates of various scholars that there were 28,000 to 45,000 *metics*, 120,000 to 170,000 free
persons (men, women, and children), and perhaps 125,000 slaves.
But this figure for the total population does not necessarily indicate
overcrowded family conditions in the city-state, certainly not in
comparison with the million or more residents of Athens in our own
time. It would be reasonable to estimate that, out of 145,000 free
citizens, there were 40,000 to 50,000 adult males who voted and
enjoyed leisure-time activities in the agora.

No respectable Athenian wife would attempt to mingle with her
husband and his female companions in the agora. Similarly, no respectable Athenian husband would try to conduct his business affairs at home instead of in the marketplace. Consequently, Socrates
is always pictured teaching in the agora, and Aristotle is always
portrayed lecturing to students in his university outdoors. In the
eighth century B.C. the poet Hesiod had noted that for the Athenian
citizen the main requirements of life were a house, a wife, and an ox

for ploughing his land; Aristotle, citing Hesiod's statement, explained the reasons for the different roles of husband and wife in family life and community affairs as follows:

Out of these two relationships between man and woman, master and slave, the first thing to arise is the family, and Hesiod is right when he says—

"First house and wife and an ox for the plough,"

for the ox is the poor man's slave. The family is the association established by nature for the supply of men's everyday wants, and the members of it are called by Charondas "companions of the cupboard," and by Epimenides the Cretan, "companions of the manger." But when several families are united, and the association aims at something more than the supply of daily needs, the first society to be formed is the village. . . .

Hence it is evident that the state is a creation of nature, and that man is by nature a political animal. . . .

Nature, as we often say, makes nothing in vain.[4]

The feeling of fellowship among Athenians, men and women alike, grew out of their shared patterns of family life and their personal friendships grounded in common moral and social standards.

A number of customs governing family relationships had become fully established, such as those relating to births, marriages, old age, and deaths. The city kept no register of births, for chronological age was of little importance, and a record was needed only by young men when they reached the age for military service. Marriage was a concern, not of the community, but of the families directly involved. The birth of a son was especially important, for he would be needed in order to "save the hearth," that is, to look after parents in their old age, to arrange the marriages of sisters, and to provide for suitable burial upon the death of a parent. The birth of a girl was deplored as a misfortune to be stoically endured. Celibacy was taboo. The death of a son was not only a tragic loss to the family but also detrimental to the community, since it left a gap in the ranks of citizens responsible for its major political, social, and cultural activities.

Numerous material and social advantages were available to the Athenian family, reflected, for example, in its daily habits, housing, food, and cultural resources, its games, sports, and dinner parties.

√ Athenians rose early, often before sunrise. After a simple breakfast of bread dipped in wine, the men usually left promptly for the agora, hurrying off like our modern urban executives who join the morning rush to their downtown offices. The houses were constructed like buttresses, with blank walls facing the street and windows opening (with no glass panes) into a courtyard. An entrance led out to the street. Many houses had two stories, in which case the dining room, normally located on the ground floor, could also be used as a workroom, but household chores were not burdensome; thus, in the absence of our modern conveniences, garbage and sewage were simply thrown out into the streets.

Produce imported from foreign lands could be purchased in the agora, but Athens was substantially self-sufficient in material goods, with its own grape vines, barley, olive trees, fig trees, vegetable gardens, and building supplies, such as stone and clay, even its own silver from mines in the Mount Laurium region of southern Attica. Athenian merchants carried on a brisk trade with many countries, importing wheat from Phoenicia and the Ukraine, iron ore from Elba, pork and cheese from Syracuse, and frankincense from Syria, and exporting wine, pottery, and weapons, shields, and helmets. Of much greater significance than these goods were the cultural contributions of Athens to the ancient world—works of a long list of creative leaders who were far greater in number and accomplishments than had ever before been known, including philosophers, historians, dramatists, poets, painters, sculptors, architects—men whose creations have inspired mankind throughout the ages. Athenians were most proud of their Dionysus theater, where they could enjoy the comedies of Aristophanes, the tragedies of Sophocles, Aeschylus, and Euripides, and they were overjoyed to display the sculpture of the great Phidias.

The Athenian citizen enjoyed community facilities and services designed to make his life comfortable and stimulating. There were barbers to trim his beard, physicians to monitor his physical health, pharmacists to provide him with medicines when needed. His daily routine included participation in athletic activities and attendance at political discussions in the agora, followed by a substantial lunch at home, and then a period of rest and relaxation. If he had no business matters to take care of, he could devote himself to reading philosophical or literary works or to cultural programs in one of three famous Athenian gymnasiums located just beyond the city gates.

The gymnasiums were elaborate institutions, centers in and near which sports and scholarly pursuits could be enjoyed, with parklike areas, gardens, and shaded walks. In these pleasant surroundings were founded the Academy of Plato, the Lyceum of Aristotle, and the Cynosarges *(Kynosarges)*, designed for use by residents unable to claim pure Athenian descent. The first of these gymnasiums, the Academy, was dedicated to the popular hero Academus, named in his honor. Since Plato taught in the garden and grove close by, his school of philosophy was known as the Academy and his disciples were called Academics. The Lyceum *(Lykeion)*, named after the temple of Apollo Lukeios and situated in an eastern suburb of Athens, was, like the other two gymnasiums, a *palaestra*, that is, a place featuring wrestling and other sports. It had been used both by Socrates and by Plato. The covered walks of the Lyceum enabled Aristotle to walk back and forth during his lectures, for which reason his renowned school of philosophy became known as the Peripatetic Lyceum.

Physical culture and athletics were regarded not only as worthwhile in and of themselves, but also as the foundation for intellectual and academic activities, the life of the mind. The young men participated regularly in vigorous sports, such as wrestling, running, and throwing the javelin or the discus, while their elders contented themselves with less strenuous efforts. After exercise in the gymnasium, the men washed limbs and body thoroughly with water supplied in vats and with soaps made of olive oil, clay, and a mixture of wood and ashes, after which an attendant poured water over them to rinse them off. Young and old alike, however, gave high priority not only to physical culture but also to philosophy and scholarship. Two of these centers of athletic prowess—the Academy and the Lyceum—were merged with schools of rhetoric and evolved into a university lasting nearly nine hundred years.

Social gatherings were not neglected. An evening formal dinner, such as the one Plato described in his *Symposium*, was a frequent occasion, restricted to male citizens. Guests would watch the shadow cast by a sundial as a guide to the prearranged time of meeting. (The term *shadow* was in fact the name given these carefully appointed dinners to which selected guests were invited.) An inferior social status was no bar to being invited to dinners run by wealthy citizens if the guest were intellectually outstanding, as in the case of Socrates, who was a lowly stonemason by trade but, on invitation by Aristodemus, banqueted at Agathon's house and discoursed at the symposium that followed.

At such dinner parties the women retired to another wing of the house while the men reclined on comfortable chaises or couches to dine. The food, served on solid three-legged tables, might consist of fish and vegetables, perhaps including delicacies, such as eels. Bread, honey, and sauces adorned the table, but, except for occasional aid of a spoon, the Athenians did not use implements for handling food at the dinner table. They shaped fingers or a piece of bread like a scoop to take up the victuals and wiped their hands with soft bread which, along with other remains of the repast, they tossed to the dogs. Before the desserts (fruits, nuts, cheeses, and cakes) were served, however, the floor had to be swept clean, and in the meantime the guests would be amused by girls playing flutes or by other entertainment. Of course, these formal dinners offering rich foods were given only by wealthy citizens. The poorer classes had to be content with less appetizing fare (perhaps barley with porridge or cakes, and salted fish with onion relish), although fruits and vegetables were plentiful in season. Among many families, meats such as veal, lamb, sausage, tripe, and blood puddings were reserved for festive occasions.

V *The Education of Athenian Youth*

Preschool education in Athens was restricted largely to play activities for boys and girls in the women's quarters of the home, using toys, such as rattles, balls, swings, and wagons—also dolls with moving limbs for the girls. The children learned to take care of pets (including dogs but no cats), and they trained snakes and weasels to trap mice. Mothers, in some families aided by slaves, were the teachers in the home.

The girls remained at home to master household duties throughout childhood, but the boys, beginning at seven years of age, went off to school daily, usually accompanied by a *pedagogue* assigned by the family to observe the pupil's progress. The schools, privately owned, charged monthly tuition fees. Virtually all Athenian boys attended school to the age of fourteen years (in some periods sixteen years) despite the fact that attendance was voluntary. Consequently the male population of Athens was almost one hundred percent literate.

For boys to the age of thirteen, the curriculum of Athenian schools emphasized reading, writing, arithmetic, and chanting. The teacher in these schools was called a *grammatist*. Reading instruction aimed at eventual mastery of the classics, such as Homer's epics, the *Iliad* and the *Odyssey*, parts of which were memorized. The pupils learned handwriting by practicing with a stylus (metal, bone, or ivory) on a waxed wooden tablet. (The stylus had a sharp edge at one end for writing and a blunt edge at the other end for smoothing out pieces of wax used for making erasures.) Later the boys would write on papyrus (sometimes called paper reed or paper rush) with a reed pen dipped in ink. An abundance of papyrus was imported from the Nile delta and made into scrolls. In arithmetic, before Arabic numbers were introduced, the Greek letters were employed as numbers (the Romans had used Roman numerals for this purpose) and the pupils practiced on the abacus.

For older boys, thirteen to sixteen years old, the curriculum emphasized geometry, drawing, music (including poems), and physical education, also grammar and rhetoric. (The teacher was called a *grammaticus*.) In the music course pupils sang to the music of the seven-stringed lyre *(cithara)* and learned to play that instrument or, in some cases, the single-reed and double-reed flute (the *aulos*). The pleasant, soft, harmonious music of the lyre appealed most to the Athenians, who considered the proper rhythms and tones (associated with poetry) conducive to the life of the soul (the doctrine of *ethos*), to dignified morality and moderation, and to harmonious character. Boys participated in varied programs of physical education, which included wrestling, throwing the discus, casting the javelin, swimming, running, jumping, and dancing. Athenians rejected military drill, boxing, and no-holds-barred wrestling *(pankration)* in the conviction that physical culture should serve the cause of personal development and enjoyment, not the objectives of war or competition.

Young men seventeen or over could enroll in university courses, which were not like our modern programs of higher education but gave them an opportunity to attend lectures of a philosopher, or a master of rhetoric and oratory, or an expert on politics, literature, geometry, legal argumentation, or science. Plato himself admitted women students as well as men to his Academy.

As early as 450 B.C., the Sophists (wise men) had made a college education available to students and had charged tuition for admission to their lectures, a practice criticized by Socrates who condemned teaching for pay as an immoral policy. The first great Sophist philosopher Protagoras had laid the foundation for the new approach to education, based on his relativistic dictum that neither the gods nor tradition but only man "is the measure of all things." The Sophist Evenus the Parian, mentioned by Socrates in the *Apology* charged his students five *minae* (about two thousand dollars) for admission to his lectures. To the Sophists, public speaking, the art of effective self-expression, was the most important aspect of university instruction and an essential requirement for success in the community. Socrates accepted some parts of the Sophist philosophy, but disagreed with other parts. Plato, however, regarded the Sophists as argumentative quibblers responsible for the ruination of Athens, and in the Academy he advocated a return to ancient values and old ideals concerning religion, morality, logic, and public service.

VI *Slavery in Athens*

More than a third of the population in Plato's Athens were slaves. The free citizens cherished their own equality and freedom, protected the *metics* to some extent under law, but denied human rights to the state slaves who labored on public works. Nevertheless, the democratic spirit prevalent among the free citizens eventually infiltrated the other social classes and ameliorated their lot to such a degree that conservative critics objected to the leniency shown the slaves. They complained that physical punishment was no longer customary, that slaves would not move aside to allow a free citizen to pass, that slaves were too comfortable, took too many liberties, put on airs, and dressed like the poor class of free citizens who might for that reason be mistaken for slaves and sometimes subjected to beatings. Roman slaveowners could put to death a rebellious slave, but that punishment was prohibited in Athens, and any slave severely mistreated could demand to be sold to a new master.

Nevertheless, slaves did most of the menial work of the city-state, often under conditions so harsh (for example, in the silver mines) that only strong able-bodied individuals could long survive. The slaves were regarded as expendable; Aristotle referred to them as "living implements." A number of slaves, however, became craftsmen, just as some *metics* and free citizens did. Socrates himself was a stonemason, and the police of Athens were actually Scythian slaves.

For wealthy Athenians the slaves performed a variety of services. Slaves would carry home from the marketplace the groceries and other purchases made by their master. They would accompany him on a journey to dinner parties; returning at night, they would lead the way with torches or horn-lanterns and help the master perambulate if he were drunk. However, Athenians were temperate by nature and usually, even at dinner parties, watered their wine, mixing three parts of water to two parts of wine. A dinner party was the setting for Plato's *Symposium*, a term referring to a discussion following the presentation of papers by individuals participating in a seminar, but meaning literally drinking together, with overtones of conviviality and entertainment, hence a drinking party. (Plato's *Symposium* is an exquisitely written dialogue containing speeches about love.) Drunkenness was frowned upon; the drunkard was made the butt of jokes, subjected to ridicule in contemptuous terms, such as "dipped" and "wet."

As previously mentioned, the slaves often served as *pedagogues*, accompanying the boy to school and supervising his daily life. The Greek word *pedagogue* (which meant literally going on foot) at first referred to a tutor and travelling companion, later to a teacher.

Plato's attitude toward slavery is evident in his philosophical writings. More than two thousand years before Patrick Henry pleaded, "Give me liberty or give me death," Plato wrote, "Fear slavery more than death."[5] In his dialogue, the *Laws*, Plato elaborated on his views concerning the proper treatment of slaves: "We should tend them carefully, not only out of regard to them, but yet more out of respect to ourselves. And the right treatment of slaves is to behave properly to them, and to do to them, if possible, even more justice than to those who are our equals; for he who really and naturally reverences justice, and hates injustice, is discovered in his dealings with any class of men to whom he can easily be unjust."[6]

26 PLATO

VII   *Fair Play in Athens*

When the free citizen of Plato's Athens referred to the old style of
living, the people of olden times, he had in mind the historical
period antedating the rapid growth of cities like Athens, the ancient
era when the vast majority of people lived as farmers in open country or small villages, not yet too dependent upon huge silver mines
worked by hordes of slaves nor upon fortified walls built for defense
against foreign invaders. But agriculture on the poor soil of Attica
had declined, farmers had increasingly swarmed into the city, man-
ufacturing shops in the homes had multiplied, shipbuilding,
ceramics, and trade had expanded, and within several decades after
the defeat of the Persian invaders at Marathon in 490 B.C. the great
Pericles had built the long walls of the city. Yet Athens had no
formidable defenses excepting its superior navy and one strongly
fortified place in the Acropolis. Sparta, depending upon its highly
trained army, had not even built walls for defense.

In Plato's time Greek cities could no longer feel safe merely because their good citizens loved peace and beauty. Warlike neighbors
and foreign enemies often threatened the city-states. Nonetheless,
Athenians placed their trust in the loyalty of the free citizens. The
Spartans had a powerful army but suffered from internal divisions
which weakened its defenses. Aristotle commented that the Spartans were always geared up for war, not for peace, so that, in
peacetime, Spartan defenses rusted like a sword in its scabbard: "So
long as they were at war, therefore, their power was preserved, but
when they had attained empire they fell, for of the arts of peace they
knew nothing, and had never engaged in any employment higher
than war."[7] In Athens, on the other hand, fair play and justice,
rather than the need for defense or safety, motivated the citizens in
building their democratic society.

Fifth-century Athenians who, as slaveholders, knew the horrors
of slavery, bowed to no master, tolerated no tyrant or king. For
necessary social control they relied upon their constitution and
obedience to its laws.

Respect for law was universal. When Socrates was convicted and
imprisoned, his friend Crito offered to arrange for an escape, but he
refused. Nothing but his own decision to obey the laws and submit
himself to lawful processes of justice remained to keep Socrates in
prison. Yet, he submitted to the law and awaited execution. In 399

B.C. he became a martyr and scapegoat for the deficiencies of Athenian democracy.

The sole legislative body of the state, the *Ecclesia* or Assembly, consisted of all the free male citizens, and it conducted public business at mass meetings, including all activities of the judicial and administrative branches of government. Meeting only once each month (in addition to occasional special meetings), the Assembly had to elect a committee of five hundred, the Council, to cope with important matters beyond the capacity of such an unwieldy assemblage. The Council (more accurately called the *boulē*, pronounced "boolay") appointed the officials running government boards and departments, who served, however, at the pleasure and subject to decisions of the whole Assembly. But the boule of five hundred was also too cumbersome a body to handle the everyday affairs of the government; it delegated responsibility for such matters to a rotating subcommittee of fifty counselors, called the Prytany. These counselors were selected from the ten tribes of Attica, each counselor serving only one tenth of a year. The presiding officer of the Prytany was chosen as its chairman by ballot of its members. He held the honorary title of Head of State during his brief term of office (it lasted only twenty-four hours), and during his tenure he was required to undergo an audit and was prohibited from selling property or leaving the territorial limits of Athens. Socrates once held this position.

Inasmuch as there were no professional lawyers, judges, or district attorneys in Athens, the Assembly took care of judicial functions in addition to its legislative and administrative responsibilities. In Athens public affairs were conducted by amateurs whenever possible. An injured party found redress in justice through direct appeal to his peers, that is, his fellow citizens. Local courts administered less important trials, but serious cases, criminal or civil, were tried in courts serving the city as a whole and sitting as a jury drawn from the membership of the Assembly. The seriousness of the case determined the size of the jury, which ranged from one hundred and one to one thousand and one members. There was no judge presiding, but each jury had a chairman who acted in the same capacity as a jury foreman does in our modern courts. From the decisions of the jury, which rendered judgments of law as well as of fact, there was no appeal. The parties in a dispute pleaded their own cases (as Socrates did when he spoke in his own defense) to a jury of five hundred and one members chosen by lot. They could employ professional writers to compose their speeches, but each party had to deliver his speech personally in court. Owing to its large size, the jury could not be expected to agree upon the proper sentence for a guilty defendant in a criminal case, and for this reason both the prosecutor and the defendant were allowed to suggest a penalty, leaving the final decision to the jury.

Plato's *Apology* recapitulates numerous speeches made by Socrates in his defense. The following is a brief excerpt:

I have said enough in my defence against the first class of my accusers; I turn to the second class. They are headed by Meletus, that good man and true lover of his country, as he calls himself. Against these, too, I must try to make a defence:—Let their affidavit be read: it contains something of this kind: It says that Socrates is a doer of evil, who corrupts the youth; and who does not believe in the gods of the state, but has other new divinities of his own. Such is the charge; and now let us examine the particular counts. He says that I am a doer of evil, and corrupt the youth; but I say, O men of Athens that Meletus is a doer of evil, in that he pretends to be in earnest when he is only in jest, and is so eager to bring men to trial from a pretended zeal, and interest about matters in which he really never had the smallest interest. And the truth of this I will endeavor to prove to you.[8]

Socrates, as he expected, lost his case, but by a smaller majority than he had anticipated. The prosecutor proposed the death penalty, whereupon Socrates facetiously proposed that he be granted a reward for his teachings, the same reward the state would properly bestow upon any other true benefactor of Athens, namely, membership in the governing council, the Prytaneum. Instead of offering to accept a lesser penalty, such as exile, which would doubtless have been granted, Socrates argued that his just reward should be, not death nor exile, but freedom of the city, a prize reserved for national heroes of the Olympic games.

He [Meletus, the prosecutor] proposes death as the penalty. And what shall I propose on my part, O men of Athens? Clearly that which is my due. And what is my due? What return shall be made to the man who has never had the wit to be idle during his whole life; but has been careless of what the many care for—wealth, and family interests, and military offices, and speaking in the assembly, and magistracies, and plots, and parties. Reflecting that I was really too honest a man to be a politician and live, I . . . sought to persuade every man among you that he must look to himself, and seek virtue and wisdom before he looks to his private interests; and look to the state before he looks to the interests of the state; and that this should be the order which he observes in all his actions. What shall be done to such an one? Doubtless some good thing, O men of Athens, if he has his reward; and the good should be of a kind suitable to him. What should be a reward suitable to a poor man who is your benefactor, and who desires leisure that he may instruct you? There can be no reward so fitting as maintenance in the Prytaneum.[9]

Notwithstanding the fact that the major pre-Socratic philosophers were all guilty of the same crime, impiety, with which Socrates was charged, only four were prosecuted, and of these four only Socrates was sentenced to death. Although the verdict on Socrates was tragic, the failure to prosecute various other major philosophers bears witness to wide interest among the people in justice and in the toleration of dissenting ideas.

VIII *Solon's Contributions to Athenian Democracy*

The aforementioned characteristics of Athenian democracy developed over a period beginning two centuries before Plato's Academy (founded in 387 B.C.). The great poet and conservative reformer Solon (ca. 638–559 B.C.) must be credited with the honor of initiating the movement for democratic liberties. He abolished enslavement of the poor for debt and gave members of lower classes a taste of justice and fair play, and even some share in the government. From these beginnings evolved eventually the full-blown democracy which enabled Pericles (Head of State from 460 B.C. until his death from the Plague in 429 B.C.) to declare boastfully to fellow Athenians:

We lead a life of freedom not only in our politics but in our mutual tolerance of private conduct. We do not resent our neighbor doing what he pleases, nor subject him to those marks of disapproval which poison pleasure though they may inflict no formal injury; and while our private intercourse is thus free from constraint, this does not react to the detriment of law and order, which are preserved by a wholesome respect for the constituted authorities and for the laws of the land, especially those which protect the victims of injustice and those whose moral sanction is so strong that there is no need for them to be written.[10]

Solon was elected Archon (Chief of State) in 594 B.C. His unprec-
edented reforms—so unique that his name has become a synonym
for a member of a legislature—were both economic and constitutional. They included *seisachtheia*, that is, the cancellation of all
public and private debts—thereby setting free many individuals
who had been imprisoned or enslaved because of past financial
indebtedness—and also ending the practice of loaning money to
borrowers who offered themselves as collateral. New laws on inheri-
tance stipulated that inherited wealth must be passed on to all the
heirs (instead of solely to wealthy widows), thus helping to break up
the largest estates of the rich, whose lands, however, were never
confiscated nor turned over unjustly to the poor. Solon's major constitutional reforms, justifying his reputation as the aristocratic
champion of the people and founder of Athenian democracy, included reorganization of the people's ancient Assembly (the
Ekklesia), broadening its membership, and formation of a new
council or committee of the Assembly (the *boulē*). The boule, which
had five hundred members representing ancient tribes, prepared
laws for submission to the Assembly. Subcommittees, the *Prytaneis*,
were added later, probably in 510 B.C. by the democratic statesman
Cleisthenes. Creation of new courts of justice, the *Heliaea*, may
have been Solon's greatest reform. Members of the Assembly
served as the jurors in the *Heliaea*. Any free citizen who felt that a
magistrate had rendered an unjust decision could appeal to these
new courts for redress. Two centuries afterward, this reform enabled Socrates to defend himself before a body of democratic jurors,
and politicians who, however, finally convicted him.

In Solon's democracy, even though sovereign power was shifted
from the magistrates and old aristocratic council or boule of the
Areiopagos to the populace as a whole, the wealthy classes retained
a superior political status. Solon divided the population into four
classes: (1) the *Pentacosiomedimnoi* (the wealthiest landowners who
paid the highest taxes to the state because their lands produced the
largest quantities of grain, oil, and wine); (2) the *Hippeia* (the
horsemen, who had to contribute a war-horse for use by the state);
(3) the *Zeugitai* (the land tillers and soldiers required to serve in
defense of the state); and (4) the *Thetes* (sailors, fishermen, and
artisans, who were not allowed to hold public office). Plato's political
masterpiece, the *Republic*, written two centuries later, advocated
the division of the population into three classes: guardians, warriors,
and artisans.

CHAPTER 2

Plato: A Biographical Perspective

PLATO, the son of Ariston and Perictione, was born into a wealthy and aristocratic family in 428–427 B.C. either in Athens or Aegina, about a year after the death of Pericles and immediately after the outbreak of the Peloponnesian War, which ended in the subjugation of Athens. His father, Ariston, who died when Plato was a child, had a distinguished ancestry that claimed descent, through Plato's grandfather Aristocles, from Codrus, the last of the line of the kings of Athens. Plato's mother traced her genealogy to Solon, whose achievements as archon and founder of Athenian democracy have been previously noted. Her brother Charmides and her cousin Critias were both members of the oligarchy of the Thirty Tyrants designated by Sparta to govern Athens at the close of the Peloponnesian War. Critias was a descendant of Dropides, a relative of Solon.

Plato had two older brothers, Adeimantus and Glaucon, mentioned in the *Republic*, and a sister Potone, mother of Speusippus, who succeeded him as head of the Academy. Plato's widowed mother Perictione married her uncle, Pyrilampes, an intimate friend and supporter of Pericles who presided (461–429 B.C.) over the Golden Age of Athens. Perictione had another son, by Pyrilampes, named Antiphon, about whom Plato wrote in the introduction to the *Parmenides* that he "nowadays takes after his grandfather of the same name and devotes most of his time to horses." Plato, who remained a lifelong bachelor, died in 347 B.C. at eighty years of age while attending a marriage feast or birthday celebration and was buried in the Academy.

Plato has been so idealized that it is exceedingly difficult to separate legend from fact in order to penetrate the Platonic myth and discover the real or historic Plato. The Greeks did not apply the historic method to the biographies of individuals. Doubtless, the entire chronology of Plato's life is made to fit a scheme (invented by the Alexandrian librarian, Appolodorus) wherein the lifetime of an individual was divided into four periods of twenty years each. Hence, "Plato met Socrates at the age of twenty, established his Academy at the age of forty, went to Syracuse at the age of sixty, and died at the age of eighty."[1] Even the eminent pioneering conscientious scholar on Plato, Eduard Zeller, can only make conservative assumptions about his career, based upon what is known about Athens in the fifth century B.C.

I *The Early Years*

In his youth, Plato was instructed by eminent teachers in grammar, music, and gymnastics; and he reportedly distinguished himself in athletics by competing in the Isthmian games for a prize. "That he early learned to ride goes without saying; his brothers were troopers, we must believe the same of him, and he had at his command the most accurate knowledge of the bodily build of a noble steed,"[2] wrote Wilamowitz-Moellondorf, one of Plato's biographers. As an Athenian youth of military age, Plato served in the armies of Athens (because of his social status in the cavalry instead of the infantry) during the final years of the Peloponnesian War when Athens was in urgent need of manpower.

Aristotle informs us that "from his youth upward Plato had been familiar with Cratylus and with the opinions of the Heraclitian School."[3] Plato also had literary aspirations directed particularly toward creative work in poetry and tragedy. He seemed destined to pursue a public career until he became a disciple of Socrates. An eager student of philosophy under the guidance of Socrates, Plato became thoroughly familiar with the complex problems of the discipline and taught his own students the value of philosophical examination of every moral and political opinion. In his Seventh Letter, Plato mentions that in his youth he entertained the hope of entering upon a political career as soon as he came of age, but the abuses perpetrated by the Thirty Tyrants and the death of Socrates aborted this aspiration.

II *Plato's Eight Years with Socrates*

It is assumed that Plato was twenty when he met Socrates and remained his faithful disciple not only throughout the lifetime but also after the death of Socrates. Plato's uncle Charmides and cousin Critias, however, had been close friends of Socrates even before Plato was born. Unfortunately, during the following eight years to the time of his master's death in 399 B.C., his relationship of philosophical dialogue with Socrates had many serious disruptions because of wars and other disorders in the land. In 406 B.C., Socrates, as a Councillor of Athens, opposed the Assembly for acting against the law. In 405 B.C., the Spartans attacked Athens, defeating them in 404 B.C. The grim final phase of the Peloponnesian War ended in 403 B.C. when Plato was twenty-three, with the battle of Aegospotami and the surrender of Athens.

In 399 B.C., Socrates, as noted previously, was convicted on a trumped-up charge of impiety and corrupting the minds of the youth of Athens, and was subsequently sentenced to death. His accusers alleged that he corrupted the youth of the upper class, young people who were caught up in an antidemocratic current during the latter years of the Peloponnesian War. In the *Apology*, Plato represents himself as present at the trial and as one of the Socratic circle of friends, who offered to be surety for a fine proposed as a counterpenalty to the death sentence. A speaker in the *Phaedo* states that Plato was absent because of illness from the memorable gathering when Socrates drank the fatal hemlock. These are the only two facts that Plato has recorded about his own life in his *Dialogues*.

For years after Socrates' death, Plato was committed to refining and extending the Socratic principles and defending the Socratic method of inquiry against criticism. To the end of his life, Plato remained in complete agreement with the essential spirit of Socrates, vindicating Socrates' memory and perpetuating his mission.

III   *Plato's Travels*

The sequence of Plato's travels can never be known precisely, except for his journeys to Italy and Sicily, which he himself stated that he visited at the age of forty. Shortly after the death of Socrates in 399 B.C., Plato, then twenty-eight, left Athens for an indefinite stay in Megara, at the house of Euclid, founder of the Megarian school of philosophy. Citing as authorities Hermodorus (who studied under Plato at the Academy) and Eucleides (one of five foreigners present at the death of Socrates), Diogenes Laertius stated that Plato "proceeded to Cyrene on a visit to Theodorus the mathematician, thence to Italy to see the Pythagorean philosophers Philolaus and Eurytus, and thence to Egypt. . . . Having returned to Athens, he lived in the Academy."[4] According to Zeller, Plato, following the Megarian trip, "undertook journeys which led him to Egypt, Cyrene, Magna Graecia, and Sicily."[5]

Some accounts of Plato's journeys have him traveling to Persia, India, Egypt, Cyrene, Phoenicia, Babylonia, and Judea, as well as making three separate visits to Sicily (the last two when he was over sixty), a total of twelve years of worldwide travel.

During the three visits to Sicily, Plato was intimately associated with both Dionysius the Elder and the Younger, tyrants of Syracuse, and returned to Athens each time; there was a twenty-year gap between his first and second visit, when, following the death of Dionysius I and the succession of his son, Plato made an unsuccessful attempt to put the ideal of the philosopher-king into practice and convert the tyrant Dionysius the Younger into a philosopher-king.

Although Plato never reported the incident, it is said that his first trip ended with his falling into slavery, either at the order of Dionysius or as the result of being captured and sold. Eventually he was ransomed, either by Anniceris the Cyrenean, or by some unnamed friends. Although the particulars vary, the sale, assuming the story is correct, occurred in Aegina through the intercession of the Spartan, Pollis, on his way to Syracuse. The sojourn, lasting but a matter of months, occurred before 387 B.C. during the Athenian war with Aegina.

In 365 B.C., Plato was back in Athens, but by 361 B.C. he was on his third visit to Syracuse. His final attempt to translate his ideal into practice resulted in abject failure. Rather than being the embodiment of the philosopher-king, Dionysius epitomized the Socratic paradigm of the ignorant man who does not know that he is ignorant.

Following the murder of Dion in 354 B.C., Plato wrote Epistles VII and VIII justifying his and Dion's policies in Sicily. A Syracusan philosopher, politician, and brother-in-law of Dionysius the Elder, Dion (ca. 408–354 B.C.), Plato's friend and an opponent of tyranny, sought in vain to persuade Dionysius the Younger to adopt the Platonic political philosophy. Although he was regent for his nephew Dionysius the Younger, his efforts proved unsuccessful, and he was exiled in 366 B.C. About a decade later, he returned (355

B.C.) with a mercenary army of fifteen hundred men, occupied Syracuse, and made himself chief of state. His attempts to implement Plato's theory of the philosopher-king proved so unpopular that he was banished and recalled, only to be assassinated in 354 B.C.

IV *The Academy*

It was just before Plato turned forty that he undertook his travels to Italy and Sicily (and possibly Syracuse and Taras, the modern Tarento). One purpose for this sojourn was to discuss matters with the Tarentinean scientist and statesman, Archytas, a Pythagorean who inspired Plato's founding of the Academy, a new concept for an educational center.

It was on his return to Athens from Egypt in 395 B.C. that Plato bought a piece of land just beyond the city limits and, as previously mentioned, established the world's first university (in 387 B.C.) called the Academy. The Academy's primary goal was to educate citizens for statesmanship. Instruction began in a gymnasium (of Academus) and continued in his own nearby garden, the grove of Academus. The Plato scholar, W. K. C. Guthrie, reminds us that "the Academy of Plato does not correspond entirely to any modern institution, certainly not a university of modern foundation. The nearest parallels are probably our ancient universities, or rather their colleges, with the characteristics that they have inherited from the Medieval world, particularly their religious connexions and the ideal of the common life, especially a common table."[6] This appears to be the earliest philosophical school incorporated as a religious corporation formed for the worship of the muses and Apollo under fully developed corporation law in Athens.

The members of the school took their meals together and shared expenses. Plato, like Socrates, received no fee for teaching, but, unlike Socrates, he did not go into the marketplace to teach; rather, he remained aloof from the active life of the city and let the students come to him. Some scholars have assumed the Academy to be the experimental testing grounds for the curriculum of higher education outlined in the seventh book of the *Republic* and intended for the moral instruction of the rulers and citizens of Plato's ideal state.

Plato delivered lectures on special occasions both to an elite group and to a wider audience—for example, Plato lectured on the

Good using the Socratic method wherever possible (that method, of course, was not always applicable). Two of the greatest contemporary mathematicians of his time, Theaetetus and Euxdorus, taught at the Academy, where a strict and thorough training in mathematics and dialectics was the rule. The core curriculum consisted of mathematics (which included harmonics and astronomy), political theory, natural science, and biology.

At sixty, Plato had been teaching in the Academy for twenty years, and another twenty years elapsed before his death. Xenophon mentions that troops were quartered at the Academy, which was purported to have been leveled to the ground once or twice during the first century. Pausanius, a second-century writer, claimed to have located Plato's grave nearby.

The Academy, called the "University of Athens," firmly established in the Platonic tradition, endured continuously for almost nine centuries, and was glorified by Plutarch, Cicero, and Diogenes Laertius.

V   *The Dialogues*

Speaking of the threefold division of Platonic writings, Paul Shorey states:

There is now general agreement upon the broad division into three groups: the earlier, minor, "Socratic" dialogues; the artistic masterpieces of Plato's maturity; the less dramatic and more technical works of his old age. It is generally agreed that the dramatic, minor, tentative, "Socratic" dialogues are for the most part early; that the *Laws* is the latest of Plato's works; that the more arid, undramatic, dogmatic, elaborately metaphysical, dialectical dialogues form a later group preceding or perhaps partly contemporary with the composition of the *Laws*; and that such artistic masterpieces as the *Symposium*, the *Phaedo*, the *Phaedrus* and the *Republic* belong to the period of Plato's full maturity.[7]

The early group consists of nine dialogues plus the *Apology*, written shortly after Socrates' death as a memorial to him, of which Socrates is always the central figure. Employing the Socratic method, Plato vigorously exposes the ignorance of the alleged expert, the politician, the military general, the priest, or the poet, while commending the craftsman. Through the inductive method, he arrives at universal definitions.

VI *The Letters*

A collection of thirteen letters attributed to Plato and extant during the first century A.D., was included by the scholar Thrasyllus, a
contemporary of the Emperor Tiberius, in his complete edition of
Plato's works. From our knowledge of early Platonic scholars, it is
evident that they accepted these letters as genuine, but contemporary scholars have long debated their authenticity; although some
repudiate all of them, most accept only the seventh and eighth
letters as authentic. Charles M. Bakewell has classified the letters
into the following three groups on the basis of the persons to whom
they are addressed: (1) letters to Dionysius (1–3, 13); (2) letters to
Dion and Dion's friends (4, 7–8, 10); (3) letters to various rulers and
statesmen (5–6, 9, 11–12).

Eight of the thirteen letters, including the celebrated seventh,
concern Sicilian rulers, Dion and Dionysius. The letters represent
an ancient tradition within a century of Plato's time, and they report
salient historical and biographical details pertaining to the practical
activity of Plato and the political influence of the Academy.

The epistle as a special literary type was well established as early
as the second century B.C. and the "open" letters, comparable to an
oration or dialogue and intended for publication, had an excellent
chance of preservation. The only two letters, which can with considerable confidence be accepted as genuine are two "open" letters,
namely, the seventh and the eighth, the longest, most salient, and
most informative. Letter seven is mainly autobiographical, outlining
the stages of Plato's development and concentrating on his role in a
violent, historical episode of fourth-century Syracusan politics.
Whether the letter is genuine or the work of one of his immediate
disciples, it remains of the greatest historical value, since it was
either written before or soon after Plato's death. It gives insight into
Plato's motives and vindicates his actions. Spurious or genuine,
notwithstanding, the seventh and eighth letters are the only real
source of information about Plato's career and his abortive attempt
to set up an ideal state in Syracuse with Dionysius as philosopher-
king. Although we know virtually nothing about Plato from his contemporary writers, his writings, a priceless heritage, were carefully
and reverently preserved intact in the Academy.

CHAPTER 3

Psychology and Personality Theory

THERE are many striking parallels between the psychology of Plato and that of Sigmund Freud. Both lay heavy stress on the irrational in the human being; both emphasize an erotic impulse; both offer a triune structure of the personality with elements of the personality that are amazingly similar; both view the rational (conscious ego) as the executive of the personality; both emphasize (if not overemphasize) the role of sex in personality motivation; the two lay great stress on the unconscious mind; the two underscore the psychological association of ideas and experiences; both men cite the mechanism of identification; and they both share views on dreams, dream interpretation, and a mechanism that Freud termed the censor. The resemblances of the two psychological systems do not end here, for other comparisons are readily made, such as the mechanism of sublimation, catharsis, abreaction, and unconscious motivation.

I Eros: Fundamental Human Motivation

The fundamental generative impulse for Plato was *eros* ("love" or "desire"). It accounts for all stages of love, from sexual to philosophical or *Platonic love*. The impulse to philosophize, held Plato, is *mania*, that is, enthusiasm or inspiration. The Greek word *mania* means frenzy and is used to depict religious and artistic inspiration. When perception of copies in the earthly world awaken the remembrance of the world of Ideas, one is possessed with wonderment, excited with delight, and transported in ecstasy. "Wonder," exclaimed the Socratic Plato, "is the feeling of a philosopher, and philosophy begins in wonder."[1]

Ideal enthusiasm, as well as sexual desire, was regarded by Plato as a form of love. The same holds true for physical or sensuous beauty and celestial beauty. Listen to Socrates as Plato puts these perceptive observations and words into his mouth regarding beauty and love, including sexual beauty and sexual love.

But of beauty, . . . we saw her there shining in company with the celestial forms; and coming to earth we find her here too, shining in clearness through the clearest aperture of sense. For sight is the most piercing of our bodily senses; though not by that is wisdom seen; her loveliness would have been transporting if there had been a visible image of her, and the other Ideas, if they had visible counterparts, would be equally lovely. But this is the privilege of beauty, that being the loveliest she is also the most palpable to sight. Now he who is not newly initiated or who has become corrupted does not easily rise out of this world to the sight of true beauty in the other; he looks only at her earthly namesake, and instead of being awed at the sight of her, he is given over to pleasure, and like a brutish beast he rushes on to enjoy and beget; he consorts with wantonness, and is not afraid or ashamed of pursuing pleasure in violation of nature. But he whose initiation is recent, and who has been the spectator of many glories in the other world, is amazed when he sees any one having a god-like face or form, which is the expression of divine beauty; and at first a shudder runs through him, and again the old awe steals over him. . . . There is a sort of reaction, and the shudder passes into an unusual heat and perspiration; for, as he receives the effluence of beauty through the eyes, the wing moistens and he warms. . . . During this process the whole soul is all in a state of ebullition and effervescence. . . . The soul is beginning to grow wings, the beauty of the beloved meets her eye, and she receives the sensible warm motion of particles which flow towards her, therefore called emotion, and is refreshed and warmed by them, and then she ceases from her pain with joy. But when she is parted from her beloved . . . the entire soul is pierced and mad-dened and pained, and at the recollection of beauty is again delight-ed. . . . Whenever she thinks that she will behold the beautiful one, thither in her desire she runs. And when she has seen him, . . . her con-straint is loosened, and she is refreshed, and has no more pangs and pains; and this is the sweetest of all pleasures at the time, and this is the reason why the soul of the lover will never forsake his beautiful one, whom he esteems above all; he has forgotten mother and brethren and companions, and he thinks nothing of the neglect and loss of his property; the rules and proprieties of life, on which he formerly prided himself, he now despises, and is ready to sleep like a servant, whenever he is allowed, as near as he can to his desired one, who is the object of his worship. . . . This state . . . is by men called love.[2]

Note that for Plato it is eros or desire that is the basic motivation in humans, whether it be sensual desire of a wanton nature or desire for the celestial. To aspire for that which is found in heavenly realms also finds its foundation or point of origin in erotic desire. The important difference, however, is that while the former is base, the latter is highly preferred. Accordingly, Platonic love is a philosophical or intellectual impulse to unite with absolute beauty; it is a person's ascension from sensual passion to being transported to the ecstatic state of contemplating the ideal. Platonic love is also thought of as a relationship between two persons (of the opposite sex) whose interpersonal ties have transcended the sensual, resulting in the sublimation of any sexual involvement.

Eros is comparable to the Freudian concept of libidinal energy, and especially Freud's psychic energy. For Plato, it was psychic energy, a common fund of moving energy, a motivational force. As is true of Freud's libidinal energy, the Platonic eros, if it directs energy into one channel it tends to deplete it from another; that is, it must withdraw it from another. Plato explained:

As we know by experience, he whose desires are strong in one direction will have them weaker in others; they will be like a stream which has been drawn off into another channel. . . .

He whose desires are drawn towards knowledge in every form will be absorbed in the pleasures of the soul, and will hardly feel bodily pleasure.[3]

Freud referred to this phenomenon as psychic economy. The technique of attenuating if not depleting the sexual urge by shifting mental energies into the meditation of Platonic Ideas and philosophy was an important mode of sublimation for Schopenhauer, playing an important role in his philosophy. The entire process is, to be sure, what Freud later termed sublimation. The same psychic energy, eros, that winged the personality to the highest ideals is manifested in the sexual reproduction of the race at lower instinctual levels. As the energy of life, it is the motivating force of the psyche. Plato defined the soul in such terms, stating that it possessed the power of self-motion.

Eros is the yearning for immortality. The generative or procreative impulse, eros, is the sex drive or the libidinal urge, as Freud termed it, but it is much more. It is the life instinct, the human being's primary motivation, the desire to survive, the yearning to become immortal, even the longing for the good, the true, the beautiful.

Eros expresses itself in a variety of forms; its sexual expression, however, is an attempt to transform the mortal nature into an immortal one through self-propagation. Love, then, is the middle term between Being and Not-Being, bridging mortality and immortality. "It is in order to secure immortality that each individual is haunted by this eager desire and love."[4]

Ultimately, eros seeks to attain and possess the divine essence, the ideal. Physical sex is, accordingly, an image or copy of ideal love, for sensual beauty is but a replica of beauty absolute. These earth-bound copies merely replicate their heavenly prototype.

When a person loves the beautiful, his erotic impulse is desirous of the good, seeking to possess it, inasmuch as it is the source of happiness, the goal and end-all of humanity. "If he who loves, loves the good, what is it then that he loves?" queried the Socratic Plato rhetorically. "And what does he gain who possesses the good? Happiness . . . ,"[5] for by the acquisition of the good a person becomes happy. The conclusion is that love may be defined "as the desire for the everlasting possession of the good."[6] Erotic desire, then, is the yearning to possess the good with its concomitant happiness, inasmuch as happiness is the basic desire of everyone.

The generative impulse, eros, is the desire to generate something lasting. While that is its ultimate aim, the desire for immortality, in its striving toward that goal, eros, in its eagerness and heat, expresses itself in a variety of forms. Eros is procreation; it is creation; it is birth. It is more than the love of the beautiful; it is birth in beauty, because we are attracted to the body beautiful. "Because to the mortal creature, generation is a sort of eternity and immortality" and if "love is of the everlasting possession of the good," then "all men will necessarily desire immortality together with good: Wherefore love is of immortality."[7] Thus what is ultimately loved or desired by eros is immortality. "Love is of the immortal," explained Plato, "the mortal nature is seeking as far as possible to be everlasting and immortal: and this is only to be attained by generation, because generation always leaves behind a new existence in the place of the old."[8]

II *Stages of Personality (Eros) Development*

The escalation of love or eros, according to Plato, proceeds from (1) love of physically beautiful shapes and forms (sexual love; outward beauty; erotic love of physical comeliness); (2) love of beautiful souls (inward beauty; virtuous souls; moral beauty); and (3) love of the beauty of knowledge (love of beautiful sciences, that is, the search for beauty wherever it may be found); and the love of absolute beauty—the Ideal.

The three modes of beauty represent steps or graduate levels of eros or love, beginning with a sensual, erotic, or sexual love of the outward human body, and then moving toward the inward person or the love of a moral or humanitarian personality, who is capable of creating fair thoughts. Individuals, if they are to attain maturity, must arrive at a passion for knowledge; and erotic desire of a sexual kind must be replaced by an attraction for the moral realm. Thus the procedure is from a sensate realm to the supersensible or domain of the spirit. A person, desirous of reaching maturity, must catch a glimpse of beauty on each stage of human development. The proper way in which to be initiated into the mysteries of eros is

to begin with examples of beauty in this world, and using them as steps to ascend continually with that absolute beauty as one's aim, from one instance of physical beauty to two and from two to all, then from physical beauty to moral beauty, and from moral beauty to the beauty of knowledge, until from knowledge of various kinds one arrives at the supreme knowledge whose sole object is . . . absolute beauty.[9]

The three stages of ascension to absolute beauty are coordinated with Plato's three components of the human personality: the concupiscent, the spirited, and the rational aspects of the psyche. They compare with Freud's psychical apparatus (id, ego, and superego). Plato characterized personalities by that aspect of the psyche which dominated an individual. Thus, it is the Platonic version of typology. Carl Jung, by comparison, offered two types (introvert and extravert), whereas Plato recognized three basic types.

While all three aspects are found in every individual, one of the three predominates. Consequently, the person whose concupiscent psyche is preponderant will tend to be sensually oriented, his erotic development being sexually fixated. This type of personality will strive to achieve immortality through procreation, children who will perpetuate his seed. The second or spirited type looks inward for his immortality, hoping that his achievements will be recognized by posterity. The spirited are typified by military people eager for reputation, or some literary individuals hopeful that their works will survive them. The third type of personality, the rational, are characterized by a love of wisdom; their erotic development matures, assuming the form of a passion for knowledge. The latter two types of personality have successfully sublimated the sex urge or erotic desire. All three, however, are manifestations of eros. It is the third type of personality, the rational, with a passion for wisdom, that is in reach of absolute beauty and its attendant happiness. These people have made direct contact with immortality by soaring above the world of sense to the supersensible, from the temporal world to the eternal.

Further comparison of Plato and Freud will be found below; in the meantime a few more words should be stated on the development of eros. Deliberating on his phenomenology of love, Plato charted the course of love from its erotic and narcissistic beginnings by way of its altruistic midcourse to its ultimate maturity, that is, absolute beauty:

The young man who would pursue the right way to this goal must begin, when he is young, by applying himself to the contemplation of physical beauty, and, if he is properly directed by his guide, he will first fall in love with one particular beautiful person and beget noble sentiments in partnership. . . . Later he will observe that physical beauty in any person is closely akin to physical beauty in any other, and that, if he is to make beauty of outward form the object of his quest, it is great folly not to acknowledge that the beauty exhibited in all bodies is one and the same; when he has reached this conclusion he will become a lover of all physical beauty, and will relax the intensity of his passion for one particular person, because he will realize that such a passion is beneath him. . . .

Next he must grasp that the beauties of the body are as nothing to the beauties of the soul, so that wherever he meets with spiritual loveliness, even in the husk of an unlovely body, he will find it beautiful enough to fall in love with and to cherish—and beautiful enough to quicken in his heart a longing for such discourse as tends toward the building of a noble nature. And from this he will be led to contemplate the beauty of laws and institutions. And when he discovers how nearly every kind of beauty is akin to every other he will conclude that the beauty of the body is not, after all, of so great moment. From morals he must be directed to the sciences and contemplate their beauty also, so that, having his eyes fixed upon beauty in the widest sense, he may no longer be the slave of a base and mean-spirited devotion to an individual example of beauty . . . but, by gazing upon the vast ocean of beauty to which his attention is now turned, may bring forth in the abundance of his love of wisdom many beautiful and magnificent sentiments and ideas, until at last, . . . he catches sight of one unique science whose object is beauty [absolute].[10]

Note that beauty ascends in value not only from outward to inward form, but from individual to social to universal in scope. All forms of beauty have their limitation, and increasingly so as one descends the scale of eros, the only exception being absolute beauty, that is, the Ideal or Archetype. Absolute beauty is "an everlasting loveliness which neither comes into being nor passes away, neither flowers nor fades, nor beautiful in this relation and ugly in that, nor beautiful here and ugly there, as varying according to its beholders."[11]

The progressive elevation of beauty is also in the direction from fair forms to fair practices to fair notions, for love matures in this manner. The order of love's ascension as cited by Plato is to begin with earthly beauties and proceed upward toward absolute beauty. Failure to progress from one stage of erotic development to the next is termed fixation or arrested development in Freudian terminology. To revert from a higher to a lower form of development is called regression in psychoanalytic parlance.

Once contemplating absolute beauty, which Plato considers the *summum bonum*, a person will find himself living the best possible existence. "In the contemplation of beauty absolute," declared Plato, an individual will find himself in that happiest "life above all others which man should live."[12] In beholding ideal beauty with the mind's eye, the encounter with true beauty (rather than the mere image of reality) is experienced. In such an encounter a person is nourished in true virtue and thereby becomes not only God's friend but also immortal. Hence, it is by virtue of the philosophical impulse, the remembrance of forgotten Forms, that the philosophical ideal arises.

Thus the goal of eros is immortality. From an erotic sexuality or sensuality, the erotic nature becomes sublimated. The human erotic drive is the human desire or cry for immortality. Sex is a generative instinct that produces a new existence to replace the old, a perpetual process of decay and reparation, a new life replacing the old. The birth of our children extends our mortality so that countless generations provide for us a substitute immortality. "Marvel not then at the love which all men have of their offspring," observed

Plato, "for that universal love and interest is for the sake of immortality."[13] He went on to state that "those who are pregnant in the body only, betake themselves to women and beget children—this is the character of their love; their offspring, as they hope, will preserve their memory and give them the blessedness and immortality which they desire in the future."[14] Thus the sex urge is ultimately the desire for immortality. *Eros* is more than a sex drive; it is life's basic urge or motivation. Humanity's strivings, struggles, and sufferings are goaded by the desire for immortality. Ambitiousness and the motivation for achievement arise from the desire for immortality, even though the immortality produced is but spurious or substitute at best. "Think only of the ambition of men," advised Plato, "and you will wonder at the senselessness of their ways, unless you consider how they are stirred by the love of an immortality of fame. They are ready to run all risks greater far than they would have run for their children, and to spend money and undergo any sort of toil, and even to die, for the sake of leaving behind them a name which shall be eternal."[15] The desire for immortality is so intense in people that they will even settle for the mere survival of memory, though it be but a substitution for immortality.

Before leaving this section, let us reemphasize the striking resemblance of Freud's psychosexual stages of human development or his libidinal development to Plato's development of eros. Freud's libidinal urge and Plato's erotic desire are virtually alike in major respects.

III   *Structure of the Personality*

It is interesting to compare Plato's view on the structure of the personality with that of Freud. Both men structure the personality triadically; and both stress the unconscious as well as the conscious mind; further, both thinkers see the human as both rationally and irrationally motivated. The Freudian structure of personality is composed of ego, id, and superego, whereas Plato's is the rational, the spirited, and the appetitive. Freud held that a wholesome or normal person was one whose ego, id, and superego were in harmony; but Plato over two millennia ago claimed that normality was the rational, spirited, and appetitive aspects of the personality or psyche functioning in harmony.

For a healthy personality, Freud called for a strong ego functioning as the executive of the personality; but Plato long ago called for the rational psyche to superintend the other components of the personality. The ego for Freud was the rational aspect of the psychical apparatus (as he termed what Plato called the soul). While the Freudian ego is analogous to the Platonic rational soul, the id component of Freud's psychical apparatus may be found in Plato's appetitive soul. The Freudian superego was for Plato and Socrates simply conscience. Just as psychic energy is supplied by the libidinal urge to other components of the personality in Freudian psychoanalysis, erotic desire functions in a comparable manner in the Platonic system of psychology. Offering a definition of *eros*, Plato wrote in his *Phaedrus* that "the irrational desire which overcomes the tendency of opinion towards right, and is led away to the enjoyment of beauty, and especially of personal beauty, by the desires which are her own kindred—that supreme desire, I say, which by leading conquers and by the force of passion is reinforced, from this very force, receiving a name, is called *erōs*."[16]

The psychical apparatus comprises the rational, the spirited, and the appetitive. While the three aspects of the psychical apparatus or soul, namely, the rational *(logistikon* or *nous)*, the spirited *(thymos)*, and the appetitive *(epithymia)*, are essentially manifestations of eros, only the first, the rational, constitutes the intellectual nature (reason) within the personality. Although the other two, the spirited (will) and the appetitive (sensuality), comprise the irrational nature within one, the former is regarded by Plato as noble, whereas the latter is ignoble.

Neither the psychologist Ernst Kretschmer nor the psychiatrist Carl Jung was the first typologist in psychology, for Plato developed a theory of psychological types and constitutional types approximately twenty-five hundred years before either of these psychologists. Although everyone is endowed with all three aspects of the psyche, certain of us can be characterized as sensuous, others as spirited, and still others as intellectual.

Plato noted that rational types live a mainly intellectual life; they are the intellectuals of society. He called them lovers of wisdom, that is, philosophers, or men of science in pursuit of knowledge and of truth. Their pleasure is derived from intellectual pursuits. Actually all three are pleasure-seekers or are in pursuit of happiness, but whereas the rational or intellectual are lovers of wisdom and derive pleasure in their quest of truth, the spirited are lovers of honor and derive their pleasure in quest of honor; hence they constitute the achievers of society. The third class or type, the appetitive, find their pleasure in the sensual, and consequently are lovers of gain in pursuit of wealth to satisfy their sensual appetites.

Thus Plato has developed a theory of psychological motivation as well: the philosophically minded (personalities dominated by reason) are motivated by wisdom and are driven to search for truth; the spirited (strong-willed) are motivated by the achievement-motive and are driven by a craving for fame; and the sensually appetitive are motivated by a lust for gain and are driven by a mania for wealth. Each, however, is in pursuit of happiness, but because of his diverse value systems, each looks for happiness in different objectives. Explaining his observations, Plato wrote:

Then we may begin by assuming that there are three classes of men—lovers of wisdom, lovers of honor, lovers of gain. . . . And there are three kinds of pleasure, which are their several objects. . . . If you examine the three classes of men, and ask them in turn which of their lives is pleasantest, each will be found praising his own and depreciating that of others: the money-maker will contrast the vanity of honor or of learning if they bring no money with the solid advantages of gold and silver. . . . And the lover of honor. . . . Will he not think that the pleasure of riches is vulgar, while the pleasure of learning, if it brings no distinction, is all smoke and nonsense to him? . . . And are we to suppose, I said, that the philosopher sets any value on other pleasures in comparison with the pleasure of knowing the truth, and in that pursuit abiding, ever learning, not so far indeed from the heaven of pleasure? Does he not call the other pleasures necessary, under the idea that if there were no necessity for them, he would rather not have them?[17]

Which of the personality types is correct in his value judgment? Is it a matter of to each his own? Not for Plato, who appealed to the criterion of the *hedonic expert,* the term later used by John Stuart Mill. Let Plato present it in his own exquisite dialectical manner. Socrates is querying Glaucon in Plato's *Republic:*

Well, but what ought to be the criterion? Is any better than experience and wisdom and reason?

There cannot be a better, he said.

Then, I said, reflect. Of the three individuals, which has the greatest experience of all the pleasures which we enumerated? Has the lover of gain, in learning the nature of essential truth, greater experience of the pleasure of knowledge than the philosopher has of the pleasure of gain?

The philosopher, he replied, has greatly the advantage; for he has of necessity always known the taste of the other pleasures from his childhood upwards: but the lover of gain in all his experience has not of necessity—or, I should rather say, even had he desired, could hardly have tasted—the sweetness of learning and knowing truth.

Then the lover of wisdom has a great advantage over the lover of gain, for he has a double experience?

Yes, very great.

Again, has he greater experience of the pleasures of honor, or the lover of honor of the pleasures of wisdom?

Nay, he said, all three are honored in proportion as they attain their object; for the rich man and the brave man and the wise man alike have their crowd of admirers, and as they all receive honor they all have experience of the pleasures of honor; but the delight which is to be found in the knowledge of true Being is known to the philosopher only.

His experience, then, will enable him to judge better than any one?

Far better.[18]

Consequently, the intellectual that Plato referred to as the philosopher is the hedonic expert, the connoisseur of pleasure, who knows the preferred values of life, and accordingly that from which one should derive the greatest happiness and the greatest good. The criterion, however, was not merely a matter of experience, but of wisdom and reason coupled to experience. The truest pleasures are therefore the ones approved by the experience of the lover of wisdom and reason, namely, the philosopher.

Reason characterizes the epitome of being human, for it is the very essence of a person as distinct from animal forms. Furthermore, it is the rational self that renders an individual immortal. Regarding the three functions of the soul, Plato becomes ambiguous, inasmuch as on occasion the three are treated as manifestations of one soul, hence preserving the unity of personality. At other times, however, Plato gives the distinct impression that only the rational soul is immortal, the irrational (the spirited will and the sensual appetites) being mortal.

Whereas the rational psyche responds to reason, the spirited psyche or will of an individual, the second major component of the human personality, responds to ambitious pursuits. It is characterized by assertiveness, aggressiveness, ambitiousness, pugnacity, contentiousness, and accounts for a person's love of fame, glory, anger, and desire for power and victory. The spirited type of personality with his vehement will, adjusts well in a society that is militarily oriented. Hence such personalities fare well in wartime, for they respond effectively to situations demanding honor, soldiering, and traditional codes of values. Their prized values include courage, loyalty, and self-respect. Spirited types, however, do not seek to understand and comprehend values as is true of rational types, for theirs is an immediate and almost blind attachment to values. A marked deficiency of the spirited psyche renders a man effeminate; conversely, an emphasis of it in a female accounts for manliness.

The irrational psyche, comprising the spirited and the appetitive, lacks rational bounds. Consequently, the spirited psyche and the sensually appetitive self are kept within appropriate bounds by reason. The concupiscent (appetitive) soul, lacking any rational powers, is totally undiscriminating. It is, as it were, blind to values, for it is unable to perceive any (as is the case with Freud's id). "The organ of generation becoming rebellious and masterful," asserted Plato, "like an animal disobedient to reason, and maddened with the sting of lust, seeks to gain absolute sway."[19]

Within the Platonic personality structure the appetitive psyche ranks lowest, even below the spirited self (which, like it, is irrational also). The preeminent self is the rational, the life of reason. The three souls are differentiated in quality and kind as well as in rank. The spirited self not only holds an intermediate position between the rational self and the appetitive psyche, but it acts as intermediary in coercing the judgment of reason on concupiscence. Consequently, when reason is in strife with appetitive desires, the spirited will, serving the rational self, combats sensual desires. While sensual desire (appetite) resists reason (the rational component of the personality), the spirited will is inclined toward it.

Compare this personality conflict with the Freudian strife of id with ego (and superego). The conscience, Freud's superego, Plato attributed to the function of the rational psyche. Consider the following Platonic dialogue:

> And might a man be thirsty, and yet unwilling to drink?
> Yes, he said, it constantly happens.
> And in such a case what is one to say? Would you not say that there was something in the soul bidding a man to drink, and something else forbidding him, which is other and stronger than the principle which bids him?

I should say so.

And the forbidding principle is derived from reason, and that which bids and attracts proceeds from passion and disease?

Clearly.

Then we may fairly assume that they are two, and that they differ from one another; the one with which a man reasons, we may call the rational principle of the soul, the other, with which he loves and hungers and thirsts and feels the flutterings of any other desire, may be termed the irrational or appetitive, the ally of sundry pleasures and satisfactions?

Yes.[20]

While the rational aspect of the soul employs the vehicle of concepts to attain its scientific knowledge, the appetitive soul resorts to perception which yields opinion at best but never any genuine knowledge. Essentially, it is chiefly the perception of pleasure and pain that Plato has in mind. Nevertheless, even the appetitive aspect of the personality has its cognitive side. Thus Plato's is a *cognitive psychology*, for we do not merely sense the world around us but perceive it actively, that is, with cognition. Self-consciousness, however, is attributed to the rational psyche, and it is the rational self that is the real seat of personality.

Motivations are rationalistic and hedonistic. The human being is not only enticed by pleasure, but is fascinated by reason, the clash of the two often proving a source of mental conflict and anguish. Thus a person is pulled in opposing directions and thereby subjected to tensions because of conflicting aspects of the psyche. The concupiscent psyche occasionally runs counter to reason, or that part of the psyche that Freud termed the ego. In Freudian terminology, the ego clashes with the id. While a person's immortal nature inclines him toward the good, his mortal soul is attracted toward pleasure and its concomitant evil. Plato explains this as follows:

Every one sees that *eros* is a desire, and we know also that non-erotics desire the beautiful and good. Now in what way is the erotic to be distinguished from the non-erotic? Let us note that in every one of us there are two guiding and ruling principles which lead us whither they will; one is the natural desire of pleasure, the other is an acquired opinion which aspires after the best; and these two are sometimes in harmony and then again at war, and sometimes the one, sometimes the other conquers. When opinion by the help of reason leads us to the best, the conquering principle is called temperance; but when desire, which is devoid of reason rules in us and drags us to pleasure, that power of misrule is called excess. . . . The desire of eating, for example, which gets the better of the higher reason and the other desires, is called gluttony . . . ; the tyrannical desire of drink, which inclines the possessor of the desire to drink, has a name which is only too obvious.[21]

The instinctual urge or irrational desire propelling such behavior, Plato identified as eros. Eros, a surd of human nature, is accounted for by Plato's factor of *anagkē* ("necessity").

The human predicament consists of the fact that a person is not only a rational being but is an animal being with animal appetites and desires. While the passions of sensuality appear to be invariably appropriate for animals, the same does not hold for humans. Furthermore, appetite is insatiable because of the impossibility of true satisfaction. Appetite proceeds endlessly in a constant state of flux without providing genuine satisfaction. Later, Arthur Schopenhauer grounded his entire philosophy of irrationalism on this Platonic observation. Consequently, any attempt to fulfill human appetitive desires is futile: the hedonist cannot escape his world of illusion. Physical pleasures are not as authentic as mental ones, for they are less real. The objective of the hedonist is pleasure, but pleasure per se is merely appetite in a state of satisfaction. Hence there is no object to pleasure, for it is essentially subjective.

Plato explained the pleasure of sensual appetite in terms of what Freud later termed repetition compulsion. Appetite, being bipolar, oscillates between painful deprivation and the elimination of appetite. Intense appetite, a painful experience, is alleviated when its cause—deprivation—is removed. The feeling of relief, then, is what a person experiences in concupiscent pleasures and confuses with a genuine object that can be labeled pleasure. Accordingly, pleasure is simply the absence of pain, the removal of deprivation, whether sex deprivation or food deprivation (hunger). Consequently, it is impossible to remain continuously happy—that is, from a sensual or hedonistic standpoint. Consider Plato's view:

Is not pleasure opposed to pain?
True.
And there is a neutral state which is neither pleasure nor pain?
There is.
A state which is intermediate, and a sort of repose of the soul about either. . . . After all nothing is pleasanter than health. But then they never knew this to be the greatest of pleasures until they were ill. . . . And when

persons are suffering from acute pain, you must have heard them say that there is nothing pleasanter than to get rid of their pain? . . . And there are many other cases of suffering in which the mere rest and cessation of pain, and not any positive enjoyment, is extolled by them as the greatest pleasure? . . . Again, when pleasure ceases, that sort of rest or cessation will be painful?

Doubtless, he said.

Then the intermediate state of rest will be pleasure and will also be pain? So it would seem. . . .

How, then, can we be right in supposing that the absence of pain is pleasure, or that the absence of pleasure is pain?

Impossible.

This then is an appearance only and not a reality; that is to say, the rest is pleasure at the moment and in comparison of what is painful, and painful in comparison of what is pleasant; but all those representations, when tried by the test of true pleasure, are not real but a sort of imposition?

That is the inference. . . .

Still, the more numerous and violent pleasures which reach the soul through the body are generally of this sort—they are reliefs of pain.[22]

Only the pleasures of appetite are deceptive rather than all pleasures. Unlike sensual and appetitive pleasure, true and pure pleasures are not relative but absolutely good. The sensual are but their shadows. The true are pursued by the wise.

IV *The Psychology of Dreams*

Long before Freud deliberated on the psychology of dreams, the interpretation of dreams, dreams as wish fulfillment, and dreams as psychic expressions of the id, Plato was discussing the matter with uncanny insight. Appetites, which were successfully curbed during one's waking hours, could rage unharnessed in dreams. This phenomenon, termed by Freud wish fulfillment, was Plato's way of calling attention to the bestial nature dormant in a person, and quickened in the dream state. Apparently, neither one's rational powers nor the laws of the state are able to restrain and contain appetitive desires and sensual urges that erupt in one's dream world. In the records of Plato, we read:

Certain of the unnecessary pleasures and appetites I conceive to be unlawful; every one appears to have them, but in some persons they are controlled by the laws and by reason, and the better desires prevail over them—either they are wholly banished or they become few and weak; while in the case of others they are stronger, and there are more of them.

Which appetites do you mean?

I mean those which are awake when the reasoning and human and ruling power is asleep; then the wild beast within us, gorged with meat or drink, starts up and having shaken off sleep, goes forth to satisfy his desires; and there is no conceivable folly or crime—not excepting incest or any other unnatural union, or parricide, or the eating of forbidden food—which at such a time, when he has parted company with all shame and sense, a man may not be ready to commit.[23]

Freud used the term censor to denote that which prevents us from even daring to dream of certain things mentioned by Plato, such as incest and parricide.

Plato does, nevertheless, recommend a technique for coping with the antisocial character of dreams. First, he advised suitable preparation for sleep by saturating the mind with wholesome thoughts. But it is also necessary to practice moderation, allowing the appetites some discretionary satisfactions. Explaining his position on the psychic expression of inordinate sensual appetites during dreams, Plato wrote:

When a man's pulse is healthy and temperate, and when before going to sleep he has awakened his rational powers, and fed them on noble thoughts and enquiries, collecting himself in meditation; after having first indulged his appetites neither too much nor too little, but just enough to lay them to sleep, and prevent them and their enjoyments and pains from interfering with the higher principle—which he leaves in the solitude of pure abstraction, free to contemplate and aspire to the knowledge of the unknown, whether in past, present, or future: when again he has allayed the passionate element, if he has a quarrel against any one—I say, when after pacifying the two irrational principles, he rouses up the third, which is reason, before he takes his rest, then, as you know, he attains truth most nearly, and is least likely to be the sport of fantastic and lawless visions.[24]

Plato is here asserting that there are id urges, as Freud would say, in even the finest people. "The point I desire to note," wrote Plato, "is that in all of us, even in good men, there is a lawless wild-beast nature, which peers out in sleep."[25] These animal appetites are not due to faulty rearing, for they are as much a part of our nature as are our noble characteristics. Plato observed that corresponding to the three fundamental types of life (vegetable, animal, and rational) there are three natures in a human being. Since each is an aspect of a person's soul, it is impossible to rid oneself of any, for an individual is a unity, who shares features with the vegetative and animal kingdom. Only the rational self is a singularly human quality and constitutes the immortal self. The most that one can do with the irrational aspects of the personality, such as sensuality, is to bridle it, thereby allowing it only rational expression. It is the supernal aspect of the personality, the rational self, that (with the force exerted by the spirited will) keeps the sensual appetites in containment.

Although Plato strove a lifetime to establish the doctrine of the freedom of the will, he was never able to free himself from the Socratic theory of an intellective will, a will directed by reason. Thus Plato's cognitive psychology even penetrates his theory of free will. Even the Kantian doctrine of the autonomy of the will fell into the clutches of cognitivism, for Kant allowed only for a rational free will. The intellectualist St. Thomas Aquinas made will subservient to the intellect, and Benedict Spinoza was virtually Socratic in adopting an intellective will. The upshot of the matter is that a person will not knowingly do wrong, an assumption which attributes evil to ignorance rather than choice. Since people are by nature good, evil is to pursue the good but fail, to aim at the good but to miss. Evil then is frustration. The person who actually desires evil is not cognizant or appreciative of its pernicious character.

V Catharsis and Sublimation

The phenomena of catharsis and sublimation were first considered by Plato (long before Freud emphasized them in his own researches) and received the attention of Plato's disciple, Aristotle. The term *catharsis*, of Greek origin, means cleansing, but in our context and in contemporary psychology it connotes an emotional cleansing. The process of sublimation is the channeling and expression of socially disapproved feelings in a socially acceptable manner.

Plato noted that the emotions which we are ashamed to display in public regarding our own personal lives receive free vent when we attend the theater or read plays. The repressed feelings under these conditions are poured out and cleansed from our systems because social taboos regarding their expression do not hold under these social circumstances. Although the term catharsis—signifying emotional cleansing—was coined by Aristotle, it was Plato who first discussed the phenomenon. Speaking of the playwriters, Plato asserted:

The best of us . . . when we listen to a passage of Homer, or one of the tragedians, in which he represents some pitiful hero who is drawling out his sorrows in a long oration, or weeping, and smiting his breast—the best of us, you know, delight in giving way to sympathy, and are in raptures at the excellence of the poet who stirs our feelings most. . . . But when any sorrow of our own happens to us, then you may observe that we pride ourselves on the opposite quality—we would fain be quiet and patient; this is the manly part, and the other which delighted us in the recitation is now deemed to be the part of a woman.[26]

Unlike Aristotle and Freud, however, Plato did not condone catharsis, for he felt that it merely reinforced the weaker side of a person's nature. Catharsis, rather than cleansing the emotions from a personality, would through the sympathic induction of emotion create a genuine weakness in one's confronting reality. Plato does not approve of this form of sublimation, for he writes:

When in misfortune we feel a natural hunger and desire to relieve our sorrow by weeping and lamentation, and that this feeling which is kept under control in our own calamities is satisfied and delighted by the poets;—the better nature in each of us, not having been sufficiently trained by reason or habit, allows the sympathetic element to break loose because the sorrow is another's; and the spectator fancies that there can be no disgrace to himself in praising and pitying any one who comes telling him what a good man he is, and making a fuss about his troubles; he thinks that the pleasure is a gain.[27]

The serious objection Plato harbors is that "few persons ever reflect . . . that from the evil of other men something of evil is communicated to themselves. And so the feeling of sorrow which has gathered strength at the sight of the misfortunes of others is with difficulty repressed in our own."[28]

The same holds true for other passions, including lust, anger, and the like. The theater merely "feeds and waters the passions instead of drying them up." They should be harnessed under reasonable control. Although this aspect of Plato's thinking would be objectionable to Freud, another contemporary distinguished psychologist, Gordon W. Allport, would agree with Plato. For according to

Allport's theory of functional autonomy, the promiscuous display of emotions may develop them to a point of self-motivation without a reasonable cause.

VI   *The Association of Ideas*

In psychology the doctrine of the association of ideas does not stem from John Locke, though he did in fact coin the expression "association of ideas." It evidently arises from Platonic psychology. Plato was well aware that one idea leads to another, and that to still another, the chain continuing sometimes indefinitely. Terming the phenomenon "recollection," Plato rhetorically inquires:

What is the feeling of lovers when they recognize a lyre, or a garment, or anything else which the beloved has been in the habit of using? Do not they, from knowing the lyre, form in the mind's eye an image of the youth to whom the lyre belongs? And this is recollection. In like manner any one who sees Simmias may remember Cebes; and there are endless examples of the same thing.

Endless, indeed, replied Simmias.

And recollection is most commonly a process of recovering that which has been already forgotten through time and inattention.

Very true, he said.

Well; and may you not also from seeing the picture of a house or a lyre remember a man? and from the picture of Simmias, you may be led to remember Cebes.[29]

In the process of psychoanalysis, Freud also had much to do with the association of ideas. But Freud's interest was in the "free association of ideas," his view being that ideas, in freely flowing together, would eventually lead one to the basic, pertinent idea involved in emotional distress. As a psychology, however, associational psychology should be credited to Plato; at least his psychology should be recognized as the antecedent of contemporary psychological theories of association.

VII   *Psychological Adjustment:*
The Principle of True or Proper Form

Normality consists in being one's true self, while abnormality is a deviation from one's proper form or self. The more a person is true to himself, the more adjusted he is. Furthermore, a great deal more disruption is required to adversely affect the person in his perfect state than one who deviates from it. That is to say, greater tensions can be absorbed by the normal person than by the abnormal one. To the extent to which a person deviates from his norm, to that extent his defenses are subject to collapse. On the other hand, a healthy person has a much higher frustration level as well as a higher level of coping with other adverse factors.

The closer one is to perfection, the less likely is he to depart from it, perfection being his true self or proper form. Consider Plato's argument: "Is it not true, then, that things in the most perfect condition are the least affected by changes from outside? Take the effect on the body of food and drink or of work, . . . the healthiest and strongest suffer the least change."[30] The same holds true of the personality. The strongest psyche and the most knowledgeable is least disturbed by external circumstances. This fact holds even for manufactured items, such as, for example, furniture; the better made it is the more it withstands time, wear, and adverse conditions affecting it. This state of mental health, physical health, or any other condition is attributable to its being in its true or proper form, either through nature or by training and education. Mental health, then, is obtained by withstanding external pressure. "This immunity to change from the outside is characteristic of anything which, thanks to nature or the product of craft or both, is in good condition."[31]

To possess perfect mental health is to be like God, for his divine nature is perfect in every respect, and consequently would be the last to be affected by externals. Any change in God would be a deviation from perfection, from the apex of a wholesome personality.

VIII   *Plato's Biological Psychology*

If not the founder of biological psychology, Plato must be credited as offering one of the earliest theories of biological psychology. Although Plato did not reduce the mind or personality to a physical base (as some of our contemporary psychologists do), he did localize the various components of the personality, that is, he identified some organ of the human body as the abode of one of the aspects of the psyche (or psychical apparatus, as Freud referred to personality components).

The rational component was localized in the brain, the spirited will in the heart, and the appetitive desires in the liver. He saw the seat of courage and of willpower in the heart, but heart vessels reach readily to the head and to the lower regions of the body. His theory of emotional control, it will be recalled, was that when the dictates of intelligence prove ineffective in controlling concupiscent desires, one's spirited will functions as an intermediary and auxilliary of reason to exert reasonable control over the drive of sensuality. Concerning the concupiscent aspect of the psyche, Plato asserted that this

part of the soul which desires meats and drinks and the other things of which it has need by reason of the bodily nature, they placed between the midriff and the boundary of the navel, contriving in all this region a sort of manger for the food of the body; and there they bound it down like a wild animal which was chained up with man, and must be nourished if man was to exist. . . . And knowing that this lower principle in man would not comprehend reason, and even if attaining some degree of perception would never naturally care for rational notions, but that it would be led away by phantoms and visions night and day,—to be a remedy for this, God combined with it the liver, and placed it in the house of the lower nature, contriving that it should be solid and smooth, and bright and sweet, and should also have a bitter quality, in order that the power of thought, which proceeds from the mind, might be reflected as in a mirror.[32]

The charming though allegorical manner in which Plato delivered his views aids in appreciating the point he seeks to make. Despite the diverse features and qualities that characterize a human being, a person is nevertheless a unity, a whole whose parts are carefully interrelated, both physically and psychologically or functionally.

Plato was well aware that our experience of courage involves the heart, for the spirited will builds up blood pressure. But even more striking, he points out that in the experience of anxiety in the face of danger, a situation in which courage is demanded of us, we experience the pounding beats of the heart. Such observations led Plato to identify the locale of the heart as the physiological or physical counterpart of the aroused spirit of determination, the component of the psyche that he labeled the spirited will (thumos).

Plato's localization of thought processes in the brain is quite in accord with the conclusions of many modern psychologists. His theory that this superior aspect of the psyche, reason, should have its locale in the highest point of the body was indeed appropriate, for from there it superintends all behavioral activity of the personality.

CHAPTER 4

Ethics and Value Theory

POLITICAL philosophy or social philosophy was viewed by Plato and by Aristotle as the continuation of personal or individual ethics; hence the philosophy of the group (social-political philosophy) is properly called social ethics. Whereas Aristotle, like certain other philosophers such as Jeremy Bentham, followed his ethical deliberations with his discourse on politics, Plato went further and saw the character of the state as the reflection of the ethical personalities of its citizens. Plato's state is the individual on a grand scale.

Consequently, tyrannical people with unbridled passions will create a despotic state with a tyrant as its ruler. The tyrant, according to Plato, is primarily a person who no longer has any control over his animal appetites and brutal passions. He is the victim of eros, vehement, impulsive desire. In tracing the growth of this evil force of tyranny from its beginnings in childhood delinquency, Plato observed:

He first takes their property, and when that fails, and pleasures are beginning to swarm in the hive of his soul, he breaks into a house, or steals the garments of some nightly wayfarer. . . . These in his democratic days, when he was still subject to the laws and to his father, were only let loose in the dreams of sleep. But now that he is under the dominion of Eros, he becomes always and in waking reality what he was then very rarely and in a dream only; he will commit the foulest murder . . . or be guilty of any other horrid act. Eros is a tyrant, and lives lordly in him and lawlessly, and being himself a king, leads him on, as a tyrant leads a State, to the performance of any reckless deed by which he can maintain himself and the rabble of his associates.[1]

If enough young people in the community develop evil characters, they will be able to install one of their own kind to head the state.

Even when they lack sufficient numbers, the citizenry may become enamored or charmed by these anarchists and support their rise to power. According to Plato, "When this noxious class and their followers grow numerous and become conscious of their strength, assisted by the infatuation of the people, they choose from among themselves the one who has most of the tyrant in his own soul, and him they create their tyrant."[2] Once this despotic faction assumes power, the populace must yield to the outrageous dictates of their tyrant. "But if they resist him," observed Plato, "as he began by beating his own father and mother, so now, if he has the power, he beats them, and will keep his dear old fatherland or motherland . . . in subjection to his young retainers whom he has introduced to be their rulers and masters. This is the end of his passions and desires."[3]

The same principle holds true in democratic, aristocratic, timocratic, and oligarchic states; the moral character and the psychological makeup or personalities of the citizenry determine the form of government to be instituted and the type of ruler who will rise to power.

I *Plato's Value Theory: The Doctrine of the Good*

Notwithstanding its important role in the philosophy of Plato, the Idea of Good is not sharply delineated; at least, it is not as circumscribed as we should like to have it. Good is the cause of the world, its very reason for coming into existence. If it were not for the fact that Ideas are good and that the phenomenal or existential world is good, they would not be. The relationship of the Idea of Good to the world of existence is one of purpose; hence Good is not only the etiological cause of the world's coming into being but also the purpose for its existence, the goal toward which all things tend. Accordingly, Plato has presented a teleological cosmology: the true cause of the cosmos being purpose, the phenomenal contents within it being purposefully motivated, and purpose being the Ideal of Good.

Moreover, the systematic unity accounting for phenomena working together in harmony and for the unity of substance (ultimate reality) is the Idea of the Good. The Good is the ultimate and highest hypothesis, and is even beyond being hypothesized, for the soul ascends above and beyond hypotheses to the Ideal of Good.

"The soul passes out of hypotheses," asserted Plato, "and goes up to a principle which is above hypotheses, making no use of images . . . but proceeding only in and through the Ideas themselves."[4] The Good, being simple and indefinable, is cognized by the mind's eye as it scans that region that transcends the phenomenal world into the noumenal world, and hence it is recognized by immediate intuition or direct apprehension, that is, dialectically. Plato explained:

You will understand me to speak of that other sort of knowledge which reason herself attains by the power of dialectic, using the hypotheses not as first principles, but only as hypotheses—that is to say, as steps and points of departure into a world which is above hypotheses, in order that she may soar beyond them to the first principle of the whole; and clinging to this and then to that which depends on this, by successive steps she descends again without the aid of any sensible object, from Ideas, through Ideas, and in Ideas she ends.[5]

Everything that exists, exists for some good purpose, namely, the Idea of the Good, which is the ultimate purpose. From a teleological rather than a logical standpoint, all other Ideas hold a subordinate position to the Idea of the Good. Even superior to Being (and to knowing), the Good surpasses them both. "Good may be said to be not only the author of knowledge to all things known," declared Plato, "but of their being and essence, and yet the good is not essence, but far exceeds essence in dignity and power."[6] This is tantamount to saying that the Good transcends even reality itself. Accordingly, the entire world derives not only its reality but also its worth from the Idea of the Good. It is not only the cause and creator of the cosmos but is the cosmic reason as well. Also attributed to the Idea of the Good is the Platonic principle of mixing, the union of the Receptacle (*apeiron* or "endless formless space") with the formation of that space (*peras* or "mathematical limitation") to produce the empirical world of experience (the generated world). Through its mathematical forms, space is shaped teleologically by the Idea, thereby producing the temporal world as it appears to our senses.

More than merely power, the Good is a creative force shaping the world so that it conforms to its pattern. It serves as the explanation of nature, for the existential world exists owing to its being good. Objects in the cosmos behave as they do because of the Idea of the

Good, but the fact that things exist at all is due to the Good. Even erotic desires have the Good as their objective.

As the highest Idea, the Good appears to be identical with God or the Supreme Deity, the highest goal or *summum bonum* being the attainment of likeness to God or the Idea of the Good. "Wherefore we ought to fly away from earth to heaven as quickly as we can," advised the Socratic Plato, "and to fly away is to become like God, as far as this is possible: and to become like him, is to become holy, just, and wise."[7] Happiness is to be in possession of the Good, for the Good conduces to happiness. The attainment of the Good ensues through retiring from a life of sense and pursuing a life of comtemplation. As God's purpose, the Good is the ultimate from which all else is derivative. The Good is the truly beautiful.

The Good is the motive of creation, the cosmos being an imitation, a copy, an image of God. While the ultimate end of all things is the Good, the Good is for no other purpose except itself. The Good is the valuational standard of the universe. To be perfect is to be good. Because the world of existence is as good as it possibly can be, it is complete. That being the case, the present world is the only one possible, for there can be no alternatives, inasmuch as this one is the replica of the Ideal. Hence the Good is actualized in the world as the sensed, the spatiotemporal world.

II *The Nature of Virtue* (Aretē)

Virtue for Plato connoted the power of attaining good; the achievement of moral excellence; the love and power of attaining the honorable; an internal order and a right constitution; and the harmony and health of the soul. "Virtue," declared Plato, "is the health and beauty of the soul, and vice the disease and weakness and deformity of the same."[8] In agreement with the Socratic dictum Plato held that virtue is knowledge; but later he ceased to identify it with knowledge, though he did assert that "no man does evil of his own will."

Plato saw virtue as coincident with happiness, for the two are inseparable. Accordingly, virtue is its own reward. More than being essential to happiness, virtue is the only means of attaining it.

Only the virtuous individual is free, since he is ruled by reason and is led by his own will, hence is autonomous. Perfect morality and true philosophy are identical. Inasmuch as earthly virtues are but weak copies of the Ideal, true virtue is the sole possession of the philosopher, because he is better able to contemplate such copies as they shine through the noble soul.

Socrates contended that virtue, since it was knowledge, could be taught. Furthermore, he said that virtue, being a single body of knowledge, is unitary, and that there are not a number of virtues but only a single one. One does not, therefore, speak of a virtue of courage or a virtue of justice, but simply virtue *(aretē)*. The Greek word for virtue, *aretē*, denotes excellence, and with respect to Plato's cardinal virtues, it signifies moral excellence. Accordingly, to be virtuous is to excel in some phase of the psyche (the rational, the spirited, the appetitive). The term *aretē* has also been translated to denote moral goodness, intrinsic eminence, praise, or simply, goodness.

Plato held that anything that has an end or purpose also has a virtue or excellence by which the goal is fulfilled. The objective of every person is happiness, which he attains by excelling. The psyche, then, has a virtue and a goal, its virtue being justice and its objective happiness. The person who excels in the virtue of justice is an adjusted and happy personality. Explaining the nature of ends and the virtue or excellence by which they are accomplished, Plato wrote:

Whatever, said I, the excellence may be. For I have not yet come to that question, but am only asking whether whatever operates will not do its own work well by its own virtue and badly by its own defect. . . .

Then next consider this. The psyche, has it a work which you could not accomplish with anything else in the world, as for example, management, rule, deliberation of the personality and the like? Is there anything else than psyche to which you could rightly assign these and say that they were its peculiar work?

Is there a virtue or excellence of the soul?

Yes.

Will the psyche ever accomplish its own objective well if deprived of its excellence [*aretē* or virtue]?

Impossible.

Then a bad psyche will be a bad governor and executive, and a good psyche will be a good executive [of the personality]?

Of necessity.

Then the just soul and the just man will live well and the unjust ill?

That is what your argument proves.

But furthermore, he who lives well is blessed and happy, and he who does not the contrary.[9]

Whereas Plato defined virtue in terms of excellence, Aristotle defined it as habitual moderation. To excel or to be in possession of that which is excellent is to be virtuous. The excellence of knowledge, for example, is a virtue to the person who possesses it. That reason excels pleasure in value is attested to by the Socratic Plato who "maintained that reason is far better and more excellent than pleasure for human life."[10] Human survival would fare much better relying on reason than exchanging reason for pleasure. Furthermore, the highest and truly genuine pleasures for Plato were those of knowledge and of the mind; hence without reason even pleasure is not within the human's grasp, leaving him with but spurious pleasures. Pleasures are, at any rate, counterfeit values. Concerning them Plato wrote:

Pleasure is the worst imposter in the world . . . and when it is a question of erotic pleasures, which are reckoned to be the greatest, even perjury is excused by the gods—for pleasures being presumably, like children, completely destitute of reason. Reason, on the other hand, if not identical with truth, is of all things the most like it, the truest thing in the world.[11]

Since Plato's *Cratylus* has Socrates guessing at an etymological definition of *aretē*, it might be well to add his comments to this section, despite his jesting about the matter:

I should like to consider the meaning of the two words *aretē* [virtue] and *kakia* [vice]. . . . The word *kakia* appears to mean *kakōs ienai*, or going badly, or limping and halting; of which the consequence is, that the person becomes filled with vice. And if *kakia* is the name of this sort of thing, *aretē* will be the opposite of it, signifying in the first place ease of motion, then that the stream of the good personality is unimpeded, and has therefore the attribute of ever flowing without let or inhibition, and is therefore called *aretē*, or more correctly, *aeireitē* [ever-flowing], and may perhaps have had another form, *airetē* [eligible], indicating that nothing is more eligible than virtue, and this has been hammered into *aretē*.[12]

This Socratic exposition of the term *aretē* ("virtue" or "excellence") is insightful, for it supports the ideas that the well-adjusted person is the one who excels or is virtuous, and that the personality with *aretē* is a flowing one without inhibitions impeding it. Consequently, good mental health and morality coincide in harmony. Furthermore, since virtue is productive of happiness, then the individual with *arete* enjoys happiness as an adjunct to his adjusted and free-flowing life and personality.

III   *The Platonic Virtues*

From what has been said it follows that to excel is to be virtuous. The four cardinal virtues of Plato, however, refer to the acquisition of excellence with respect to some aspect of the psyche. The tripartite personality comprising the rational, the spirited, and the concupiscent called for a concomitant virtue arising in that individual whose self is dominant in one or more of these aspects, that is, who excels in one of these three respects. Each aspect of the soul or self has its accompanying virtue or excellence.

As Plato's philosophy matured, he recognized four excellences *(aretai):* wisdom, courage, temperance, and justice. The earlier Plato had Socrates enumerate five virtues, holiness *(hosiotēs)* being added to the above four in the *Protagoras* and in the *Euthyphro.* Whereas in the *Protagoras,* holiness is but cursorily mentioned and its affinity to justice stated, the *Euthyphro* treats piety as its fundamental theme, for it is in this book that Socrates is about to be tried on the charges of impiety and corrupting the youth of Athens. While Socrates finds himself at a loss to define piety or holiness, he does point out that "the good is not good because the gods approve it, but the gods approve it because it is good." Euthyphro's definition of holiness that "piety is that part of justice which gives to the Gods their due," proves unsatisfactory, as does the definition that piety is what the gods hold dear. Plato may have assimilated holiness into his virtue of justice, for it never appeared in his later works and lost out on being recognized among his four cardinal virtues.

Wisdom (Sophia). The excellence that Plato called *sophia,* though originally meaning cleverness or skill, signifies the virtue of wisdom for Plato. It was the attendant virtue to reason *(hēgemonikon),* the rational or authoritative aspect of the psyche. The person who excels in reason is blessed with wisdom. The Greek word *hēgemonikon* also means "ready to lead or guide," "capable of command," "chief," "authoritative." In the *Republic,* Plato chose those endowed with the virtue of wisdom to be the leaders of the state.

Wisdom is not an isolated entity that may be treated as a separate and distinct virtue, but it incorporates all other virtues, hence is the perfection or culmination of excellence *(aretē)*. While virtues generally are acquired through habit, wisdom, as God-given, is innate. It is through wisdom that acts culminate in happiness. Thoughtless courage, for example, can terminate in misery, and imprudent concupiscence in devastation: "Everything that the human spirit attempts or endures, when under the guidance of wisdom, ends in happiness." The Platonic Socrates added: "If virtue is a characteristic of the personality, and is admitted to be beneficial, it must be wisdom, for none of the things of the soul are either profitable or hurtful in themselves, but become advantageous or harmful by the addition of wisdom or folly; and therefore if virtue is advantageous, virtue must be some sort of wisdom."[13]

Because of its participation in truth, beauty, and symmetry— three elements of the Good—wisdom is nearer to the desirable or to the Good than it is to sensual pleasure. In Plato's *Philebus*, Socrates defends the thesis that wisdom is a greater good than pleasure, for he maintained that while some innocent pleasures do have a place in the good life, the enjoyments of the mind are exceedingly more excellent than those of the senses. The experience of pleasure devoid of knowledge is like living the unconscious life of an oyster with its spurious pleasures. Socrates remarked insightfully:

If you had no memory you would necessarily, I imagine, not even remember that you had been enjoying yourself; of the pleasure you encountered at one moment not a vestige of memory would be left at the next. Once more, if you had no true judgment you could not judge that you were enjoying yourself when you were.[14]

This view is quite consonant with the classic Socratic declaration that "the unexamined life is not worth living,"[15] for Socrates' profound conviction was that "examining both myself and others is really the greatest good of man."[16]

The wise pleasures, the pleasures of knowledge, are unmingled with pain. Socrates informs us that the human mind, because of wisdom and its love of truth, will continue to seek out the Good even if the whole world should consider pleasure as the highest priority. To be wise, argued Socrates, is to be good.

Just as within the individual personality the rational psyche superintends other aspects of the personality as the executive element, those persons endowed with wisdom (since they excel in reason) assume positions of leadership in the state. Accordingly, they belong to the ruling class and are responsible for legislation in their capacity of guardians of the law. In Plato's state, which has three major classes, this group would make up the smallest of the three classes. According to Plato's philosophy, since nature, being aristocratic, has but a few among all that she produces that excel, the best are always a small minority, whether that best be people or other natural creations. Wisdom—which is God-given—is bestowed upon the few. Thus those who possess the excellence of wisdom function as the directing faculty or the mind of the state: "Then it is by virtue of its smallest class and minutest part of itself, and the wisdom that resides therein, in the part which takes the lead and rules, that a city constituted according to nature will be wise."[17]

Qualities comparable to those which guide the soul of a rational person should be replicated in the state. Just as in the human spirit the dictates of reason ought to be obeyed, so in the state the directions of those endowed with wisdom, the guardians, ought to be unquestionably obeyed by the masses. The greatest folly, wrote Plato is

that of a man who hates, not loves, what his judgment pronounces to be noble or good, while he loves and enjoys what he judges vile and wicked. It is this dissonance between pleasure-pain and reasoned judgment in the psyche that is, in my opinion, the worst ignorance, and also the greatest, since its seat is the mass of the human spirit, for the principle which feels pleasure and pain in the individual psyche is analogous to the mass or populace in the State.[18]

The excellence of wisdom, which played an important role in Plato's philosophy, was discussed in a variety of contexts. Plato held that the lack of harmony signified the absence of wisdom. Although possessed by very few, everyone fancies that he possesses it. He discussed it as the only valid commodity of exchange for which anything ought to be bought and sold. Self-indulgence, wrote Plato, "is not the right method to exchange one degree of pleasure or pain or fear for another, like coins of different values. There is only one currency for which all these tokens of ours should be exchanged, and that is wisdom. In fact, it is wisdom that makes possible courage and self-control and integrity or, in a word, true greatness."[19] Wisdom was regarded by Plato as essential to happiness, goodness, and success.

Courage (Andria). The second cardinal Platonic virtue, courage *(andria)*, is the corresponding virtue that accrues to the individual who excels in the forceful, spirited aspect of the psyche. Owing to an abundance of energy of will, determination, or willpower, this individual is said to be in possession of the excellence termed *andria*. The Greek term *andria* denotes manliness, manly spirit, manhood, or manly strength. When employed in the bad sense of that term, it means insolence. A person who excels in *thumoeides*, the spirited self, possesses the virtue of courage. In Plato's philosophy, the *thumoeides* was that part of the personality in which courage, spirit, and anger resided. He believed it to be in the heart. *Thumoeides* means high-spirited or courageous. Plato's *Republic* recommended gymnastics and physical exercise as a way of cultivating the spirited aspect of a person's nature.

The quality of courage, the theme of Plato's *Laches*, is discussed by Socrates, two celebrated generals (Laches and Nicias), and several others. They come to the realization that despite their presuming to have known what courage is, they are unable to define it because of their ignorance as to what it really is. Acting bravely, as Socrates, Laches, and Nicias have done will not suffice, for knowledge of it is a critical issue with Socrates, who places a great premium on the examined life. Socrates argues that unless the nature of courage is known we cannot advise others regarding its attainment. Laches theorizes that the person who remains at his post fighting rather than fleeing from the enemy is the courageous one. He, however, is confronted by the example of those who fight successfully while fleeing. Laches then offers the view that courage is endurance, but that too is rejected, since a person may foolishly persist in a wrong endeavor or course of action. Courage as a sort of wisdom is suggested by Nicias. But that proves unacceptable inasmuch as some animals, though courageous, lack wisdom. Nicias supersedes this definition with the view that courage is knowledge of all. But if that definition is accepted, observed Socrates, then courage, "instead of being part of virtue, will be all virtue."[20] In Plato's *Protagoras* courage is once again equated with wisdom, but it is intimated that this conclusion, though unrefuted, is questionable. When Protagoras argues that courage is confidence because the valiant are confident, Socrates rebuts the argument by showing that

those with confidence are persons who know what they are doing
and that courage is therefore related to wisdom.

Courage as the virtue complementing the spirited psyche is discussed in the *Republic*. The class of citizens possessing courage form
the state's militia, because their personalities predispose them to a
life of valor: "Everyone who calls any State courageous or cowardly
will be thinking of the part which fights and goes out to war on the
State's behalf."[21] Courage is not blind; it is not foolhardiness. Bravery is that excellence of knowing "the nature of things to be feared
and not to be feared."[22] Plato then added that the power of the
personality or of the "universal saving power of true opinion in
conformity with law about real and false dangers I call and maintain
to be courage."[23] Only a state which has a class of valiant citizens can
properly be called courageous, for the state acquires its character
from its citizens. It becomes a valorous state when a sufficient
number of its citizens develop the virtue of fortitude, a virtue which,
however, is not an unruly bravery as displayed in some restive,
hot-tempered, and wild animals, but a courage that is contained and
bound to the dictates of law and reason. "Brave, too, then," adds
Plato, "we call each individual by virtue of this part of him, when,
namely, his high spirit preserves in the midst of pains and pleasures
the rule handed down by the commands of reason as to what is or is
not to be feared."[24] Furthermore, valorous people must be gentle as
well as great-spirited. This is particularly true of those who aspire to
the guardian class and hope to assume positions of leadership in the
state. Plato was quite aware that people with high-spirited natures
are "apt to be savage," hence must be restrained and curbed by
reason and by law.

When Plato turned his attention to writing the *Statesman*,
another attempt to formulate a political philosophy, he discusses the
difference between courage and the virtue of moderation. The
courageous person has pent-up energy that prevents relaxation,
while the moderate type of person is serene. The former looks for
trouble, the latter prefers a calm atmosphere. Thus manliness and
temperance appear to be at odds with each other. "Think now," says
Plato, "of what happens with the more courageous natures. Are they
not always inciting their country to go to war, owing to their excessive love of the military life?"[25] The peace-loving class of temperate
people can bring on a war because belligerent nations, knowing that
they will meet with little or no resistance, will be tempted to attack

them. Yet both natures are virtuous and necessary to the state. Plato notes that we pay tribute to the valorous persons: "When we praise speed and energy and vivacity, whether in mind or body or the vibrant power of the voice, we express our praise of the quality which we admire by one word, and that one word is manliness or courage."[26] On the other hand, the virtue of moderation is equally laudable: "We exclaim How calm! How temperate! in admiration of the slow and quiet working of the intellect, and of steadiness and gentleness of action, of smoothness and depth of voice, and of all rhythmical movement and of music in general, when these have a proper solemnity. Of all such actions we predicate not courage, but a name indicative of order."[27] While vigor characterizes courageous behavior, control distinguishes temperate or moderate actions. Whereas actions of the former are typically impulsive, the latter are planned in an orderly fashion. Not only do people with these dual characteristics differ from each other, but these dichotomous traits are generally not to be found in the same person. Yet in the *Republic*, Plato asserted that ideally both qualities should be required of any person being considered for admission to higher education or membership in the guardian class. (Philosophers are the rare people who combine the two types of personality traits.) Plato draws a sharp contrast between high-spirited, courageous people and their more passive fellow citizens:

Facility in learning, memory, sagacity, quickness of apprehension, and their accompaniments, and youthful spirit and magnificence in spirit are qualities, you know, that are rarely combined in human nature with a disposition to live orderly, quiet, and stable lives, but such men, by reason of their quickness, are driven about just as chance directs, and all steadfastness is gone out of them. . . .

And on the other hand, the steadfast and stable temperaments, whom one could rather trust in use, and who in war are not easily moved and aroused to fear, are apt to act in the same way when confronted with studies. They are not easily aroused, learn with difficulty, as if benumbed, and are filled with sleep and yawning when an intellectual task is set before them.[28]

While each class of people (military and temperate) is vital to a nation, an excess of either one would prove disastrous. The same view is defended by Socrates in the opening pages of the *Theaetetus*.

Later in life, when Plato turned his attention to the writing of the *Laws*, he modified his views. Not only did he point out that children and animals possess courage merely as a natural gift, but he also downgraded the value of courage to the lowest position of the four cardinal virtues: "Wisdom is chief and leader of the divine class of goods, and next follows temperance; and from the union of these two with courage springs justice, and fourth in the scale of virtue is courage."[29]

To illustrate his point Plato noted that the Spartans display a typically coarse and common form of courage while at the same time they fail to show the kind of courage needed for coping with insidious desire and erotic pleasure. Resistance to pleasure requires more courage than mere endurance of pain. Plato quoted the Spartan Megilus on this point:

I think that I can get as far as the fourth head, which is the frequent endurance of pain, exhibited among us Spartans in certain hand-to-hand fights; also in stealing with the prospect of getting a good beating; there is, too, the so-called Crypteia, or secret service, in which wonderful endurance is shown. . . . Marvellous, too, is the endurance which our citizens show in their naked exercises, contending against the violent summer heat.[30]

In reply to this boast by Megilus, Plato attributed the following comment to one of his characters, an Athenian, in the *Laws*:

Excellent, O Lacedaemonian stranger. But how ought we to define courage? Is it to be regarded only as a combat against fears and pains, just that and no more? Or does it include conflict with longings and pleasures and their dangerous and seductive blandishments; which exercise such a tremendous power, that they make the hearts even of respectable citizens to melt like wax? . . .

Now, which shall we designate bad or inferior, the man who is overcome with pain or defeated by pleasure?[31]

In other words, lack of courage to withstand exotic desires is more shameful than the inability to cope with pain and hardship. The person who is able to contend with his desires displays more courage than the one who stoically endures pain but yields to temptation.

Temperance, Self-Mastery, or Self-Control (Sōphrosynē). The virtue that Plato termed *sōphrosynē* has no English equivalent.

Today we speak of temperance as if it meant a single kind of self-control or self-mastery, by which we mean moderation in sensual desires, sobriety, chastity, good sense, prudence, and discretion. The term is used to describe persons who are not enslaved to sensual desires, but display tact and sobriety.

This worthy experience of self-control corresponds to the appetitive aspect of the psyche, which Plato called the *epithumētikon*, that is, the desiring, lusting, or sensualizing aspect of the personality. Plato considered it the seat of desires and affections, its biological locale being the liver. Persons possessing this virtue or excellence are able to control their animal appetites. Thus, the virtue of *sōphrosynē* ("self-control," "temperance") derives solely through the correct rule or control of sensual appetite.

The moral significance of moderation is seen in the Greek aphorism: "nothing in excess." Although overzealous people have more intense desires and derive greater pleasure from the satisfaction of their wants, the outcome is not desirable because it makes them morbid rather than healthy. Consequently, people seeking the greatest bodily pleasures can find them only under conditions conducive to an unhealthy state of mind. Although the pleasures of wantonness are of greater intensity than temperate ones, people possessing adequate self-control "are restrained by the wise man's aphorism of 'Never too much,' and heed it, whereas the senseless profligate is mastered by his extreme pleasure, which ultimately drives him insane."[32] Accordingly, extreme physical pleasures and pains are indicative of the sick and morbid mind and body. An example of such pleasure arising out of an unhealthy physical condition is the intense feeling of relief derived from scratching an irritated skin. Contemporary psychologists (for example, Abraham H. Maslow) refer to this mode of pleasure as a deficiency need or deficiency motivation. The superior form of motivation is called self-actualization or growth motivation. In Plato's philosophy this superior mode is identified with the need for knowing and the pleasures attending knowledge. Unlike physical pleasures, the pleasures of knowledge of the mind are not accompanied by attendant pains, a point discussed in the *Philebus*.

Westerners, especially Americans, should be chagrined that they do not place more emphasis on the excellence of *sōphrosynē*, for it was the preeminent ideal to the Greeks of Plato's time. As a virtue, it has been deemphasized in the West, and this is why our language does not even have a suitable word for *sōphrosynē*. *Sōphrosynē*, the antithesis of insolent self-assertion or arrogance, characteristics considered despicable by the Athenians, indicated their awareness of the proper limits to be set for the tendencies of human nature, which was to be guided by the dictates of excellence; thus, sensual impulsiveness would be curbed instead of lapsing into licentiousness, the laws of balance and harmony within us would be respected, and excesses would be avoided.

Plato attempted without success to arrive at a satisfactory definition of *sōphrosynē*. In reviewing the arguments of Socrates in the *Charmides*, a dialogue devoted to an inquiry concerning the nature of temperance *(sōphrosynē)*, Plato recounted the following definitions of temperance: (1) Temperance is doing things orderly and quietly; temperance is quietness. (2) Temperance makes a man ashamed or modest; and temperance is the same as modesty. (3) Temperance is the practice of attending to our own business. (4) Temperance is the doing of good deeds. (5) Temperance is self-knowledge.[33]

The fifth definition was taken from the inscription of the oracle at Delphi: "Know thyself," a principle which, together with the precept that "the unexamined life is not worth living," was accorded the highest priority in the philosophy of Socrates. Despite all these definitions and discussions of temperance, including those in the *Charmides*, each definition was found wanting.

Plato's *Statesman* reiterates the doctrine of temperance as quietness that was articulated in the *Charmides*. Here, also, it will be recalled, temperance was contrasted with courage.

In the Platonic dialogue *Gorgias*, Callicles, a philosopher debating with Socrates, pleads the hedonistic cause. His thesis is that the immoderate who has indulged his erotic desires and passions completely and who finds it within his power to do so is indeed happy. Such behavior, though unconventional, is nevertheless in accord with human nature. The weak and cowardly laud *sōphrosynē* ("self-control") inasmuch as they are impotent to seize what they desire. Enunciating his philosophy of immoderate hedonism, Callicles holds that the hedonist "is to have all his desires about him, and to be able to live happily in the gratification of them."[34] He equates pleasure with the good. Furthermore, the hedonist is one "who says without any qualification that all who feel pleasure in whatever manner are happy, and who admits of no distinction between good and bad pleasures."[35] At this point Socrates contests the thesis that pleasure, regardless of its source or nature, is good, for indiscriminate or immoderate pleasures can have dire consequences. Intemperance within the personality is analogous to an unhealthy body. Just as the ill individual is in need of assistance, so is the intemperate personality. He who possesses self-control *(sōphrosynē)* dwells unfettered in happiness. Socrates further contended that pleasure and good are not identical, that it is erroneous to pursue pleasure in hope of attaining the Good. "The goodness of ourselves," argued Socrates, "and of all other good things is due to the presence of some excellence."[36] Since goodness does not arise haphazardly, it must be the result of order. Inasmuch as the ordered personality is orderly, and the orderly is temperate, it follows that the temperate person is good. Because the good person does well, he is happy. Consequently, the person "who wishes to be happy must, it seems, pursue and practice temperance, and each of us must flee from indiscipline with all the speed in his power and contrive, preferably to have no need of being disciplined,"[37] but if restraint is necessary, then self-discipline should be undertaken for the sake of happiness.

Turning to Plato's treatment of *sōphrosynē* in the *Republic*, we find it enunciated as one of the excellences of the psyche, namely, the appetitive self. The person who excels in appetitive control is said to be in the possession of the virtue of moderation, temperance, or self-control. Unlike the other two virtues, wisdom and courage, temperance must characterize all three classes: people in positions of leadership, the military, and the general public: "Temperance is unlike courage and wisdom, each of which resides in a part only, the one making the State wise and the other valiant; not so temperance, which extends to the whole."[38] Self-control should dominate not only the individual but the entire country as well. The *Republic* gives us another definition of *sōphrosynē*: "Temperance is the ordering or controlling of certain pleasures and desires; this is curiously implied in the saying of 'a man being his own master.' "[39] Hence it entails the beautiful ordering of, and restraint upon, appetites and pleasures. Conversely, the person lacking self-control is his own slave. Whereas self-control implies mastery, intemperance implies slavery.

Plato's view of the relation of temperance to the other two aspects of the psyche's excellences is not unlike Freud's theory of the tripartite psyche of id, ego, and superego. Freudian theory maintains that when the three aspects of the psychical apparatus are functioning in harmony, the personality is free from mental conflict, hence healthy. The ego, as the executive of the personality, should be dominant. Plato, reasoning similarly, explained:

It will be the business of reason to rule with wisdom and forethought on behalf of the entire soul; while the spirited element ought to act as its subordinate and ally. . . . When both have been thus nurtured and trained to know their own true functions, they must be set in command over the appetites, which form the greater part of each man's soul and are by nature insatiably covetous. They must keep watch lest this part, by battening on the pleasures that are called bodily, should grow so great and powerful that it will no longer keep to its own work, but will try to enslave the others and usurp a dominion to which it has no right, thus turning the whole of life upside down. At the same time, those two together will be the best of guardians for the entire soul and for the body against all enemies from without: the one will take counsel, while the other will do battle, following its ruler's commands and by its own bravery giving effect to the ruler's designs. . . .

We call an individual brave in virtue of this spirited part of his nature, when, in spite of pain or pleasure, it holds fast to the injunctions of reason about what he ought or ought not to be afraid of. . . .

And wise in virtue of that small part which rules and issues these injunctions, possessing as it does the knowledge of what is good for each of the three elements and for all of them in common. . . .

And, again, temperate by reason of the unanimity and concord of all three, when there is *no internal conflict* between the ruling element and its two subjects, but all are agreed that reason should be ruler.[40]

An interesting sidelight concerning temperance is provided by the *Laws*. Not only is temperance viewed as that quality that gives one control over the self, but such control and temperate disposition are acquired through a Freudian kind of sublimation. Some modern psychologists advise young people to participate in athletics as a form of sublimation in dealing with their sexual urges. Plato, aware of this problem, inquired:

Tell me then, in which case would a man find it an easier task to abstain from sexual gratifications and obey orders on the matter readily, as a decent man should—if his physique were in good condition—in training, in fact— or if it were in poor form?

He would be far more temperate when he is in training.[41]

Plato then cited the case of an athlete, Iccus, training for the Olympic games. Intensive training kept him both virile and continent. The *Laws*, which denounces homosexuality as an "outrage on nature," hence illicit, advocates moderation regarding erotic desires. Homosexuality is condemned as "a capital surrender to the lust of pleasure."[42] Moderation, declared Plato, "is dictated, to begin with, by nature's own voice, leads to the suppression of the mad frenzy of sex."[43] Believing that people are not voluntarily intemperate, Plato attributed the lack of temperance to their ignorance or lack of self-control. He asserted that the worst type of ignorance, however, is seen in the person who hates what his reason deems to be good and noble, the one who is attracted to and loves what his judgment repudiates as vile and wicked.

Justice (Dikaiosynē). The Greek term for the virtue that Plato identified as justice has often been translated to mean the same thing as the New Testament term "righteousness"; but, in the Platonic context, that interpretation of *dikaiosynē* ("justice") as righteousness does not convey the essence of Plato's thinking. The archaic term, "rightwiseness," expresses the correct meaning, as do the terms "uprightness" and "righteous dealing."

Unlike the other virtues based upon their corresponding physiological elements, the virtue of justice is a resultant of all three such elements functioning in harmony. When the rational aspect of the psyche operates as the regulator controlling the spirited and concupiscent selves so that the personality is performing as a wholesome unity rather than in discord, justice is said to emerge as the outcome. This is a major thesis of the *Gorgias*.

Although the matter is not resolved in the *Gorgias*, several notions are brought to light. In debate with Socrates, a young Sophist, Polus, assumes that an unjust person who has committed an injustice can nevertheless be happy provided that he is not punished for it. Socrates counters with an antithetical view that not only is the unjust person unhappy, but also that he is even more unhappy if he escapes punishment. Just as poverty is an evil pertaining to one's estate, and disease an evil with reference to one's body, so injustice is an evil pertinent to the mind. The disease of injustice is comparable to an incurable cancer of the soul. The happiest person, continues Socrates, is the person who has no vices, inasmuch as vice is the greatest of evils; the second happiest is the person delivered from vice through admonition, rebuke, or punishment; and the third state, that of the unhappy victim of vice, is the one caught in vice without prospects of deliverance. "He lives worst," concludes Socrates, "who, having been unjust, has no deliverance from injustice."[44] Virtue is happiness, whereas vice is misery. Although the difference of opinion is left unresolved, Polus and Socrates appear to agree on the principle that it is better to suffer evil than to commit it, for "it is not the most shameful of things to be wrongfully boxed on the ears, nor again to have either my purse or my body cut, but it is more disgraceful and more evil to strike or to cut me or what is mine wrongfully, and, further, theft and kidnaping and burglary and in a word any wrong done to me and mine is far more disgraceful and more evil to the wrongdoer than to me the sufferer."[45]

In his *Republic* (subtitled *Concerning Justice*), Plato again reviews the analysis of justice. Socrates continues his discussion of justice, insisting that the happy person is the just one, not the unjust. The nature of injustice becomes a major issue in this dialogue, but there is agreement that justice is the foundation upon which the good or ideal state is built. What justice means and how it can be achieved in the state become the overriding issues in the *Republic*. The numerous diverse meanings given to the term complicate the effort of Socrates to define justice, which, among the Greeks, could be interpreted variously as a legal right, a custom, a debt owed, a duty, honesty, fairness, right conduct, righteousness, a just dessert, or a lawful claim.

The first chapter of the *Republic* opens with the aged Cephalus venturing a definition of justice as honesty in one's speech and transactions. Justice is "to speak the truth and to pay your debts."[46] This definition is accepted as generally correct but with qualifications; for example, it would not be just to tell the truth to a madman or to repay a debt to him if the consequences would be destructive acts on his part.

Polemarchus offers the conventional Greek notion of justice as the right way of dealing with other people, namely, helping one's friends while harming one's enemies. The problem becomes complicated, however, if ostensible friends are enemies in disguise. Moreover, good people do no harm to others, not even to enemies. "Justice," Polemarchus insists, "is the art which gives good to friends and evil to enemies."[47] Justice is an art requiring skill, from the use of which, however, evil as well as good could result. The skill of a physician enables him to create as well as to cure diseases.

Although this definition of justice was common among the Greeks, having descended from the venerable sources of Homer and Simonides, Socrates took issue with it, for to harm people is to injure them, and doing injury to others makes people unjust. Inflicting injury upon another person diminishes his worth and thus makes a worse human being out of him, just as harming a horse makes a worse creature of it. Surely, this cannot be the objective of justice and right conduct.

The third definition of justice, offered by Thrasymachus, views justice as a means of advancing the interests of the strongest person or ruler, hence the doctrine of "might is right." If you possess the power, then you have the right. The ruling power decrees justice by fiat, thereby establishing a tyrannical ethic. At first Thrasymachus portrays the tyrant's status as an enviable one. As the dialogue proceeds, however, he is compelled to admit that ability and knowledge are much more important and effective than mere power as a means of enabling rulers to govern free from error. Hence *technē* ("art" or "skill") is required.

To govern or to rule is, therefore, an art. Consequently, the discussion compares the art of living with other arts and crafts. At this point the discussion focuses on virtue, inasmuch as the Greek word for virtue, *aretē*, is the same word used to express excellence or goodness with respect to any handiwork. Socrates insists, however, that justice is the necessary virtue of the state.

The important question then arises as to whether justice or injustice results in greater happiness. To resolve the question, justice is discussed in terms of excellence. To excel in one's natural abilities or capacities is the kind of justice that is profitable to society, the kind from which a person derives happiness. Inasmuch as "justice is the excellence of the soul," and since the just soul and the just man will live well, and because "he who lives well is blessed and happy," it follows that "the just is happy."[48] In his *Nicomachean Ethics*, Aristotle elaborated on this point, making it fundamental to his ethical theory, which states that through self-realization of one's true nature by fulfilling one's potentialities, each person perfects himself and experiences an attendant happiness. This is precisely the point that Socrates emphasizes in the *Republic*, a basic premise which enables Plato to define justice as follows: "That everyone ought to perform the one function in the community for which his nature best suited him."[49] In a sense this maxim could mean "minding one's own

business," that is, not interfering with others and not becoming a
misfit in the community, for to do otherwise would be an invasion of
another's rights or an encroachment on someone else's responsibilities. Unlike other virtues, justice is primarily a civic or social
virtue.

For justice to prevail throughout the country it is necessary for
the three classes of citizens to carry out their duties faithfully so that
each person will join that class of citizens for which he is by nature
suited. Hence the wise men will become guardians, the courageous
men will become warriors, and the temperate men will become
artisans, farmers, or traders. While all three virtues will to some
extent be present in all people, certain individuals excel in one
(rarely more) of these virtues. The excellence most characteristic of
an individual will determine his social class. Thus, class membership is a matter of each person's psychological temperament or
characteristics rather than his wealth, genealogy, or other factors.

If the citizens are just, the government, as a reflection of their personalities, will be predominately just. In essence, the character of the
state is a magnified version of the individual, and vice versa, the
individual is a miniature version of the government. One is a replica
of the other. The emergence of justice is not a consequence of overt
social behavior but a result of the internal order and harmony of the
personality, right conduct being the concomitant outcome of inner
order and harmony, that is, internal justice. To ask whether, under
these circumstances, justice pays better dividends than injustice is
like asking whether health is preferred to illness, for in a very real
sense "virtue is the health and beauty and well-being of the soul,
and vice the disease and weakness and deformity of the same."[50]

The high estimation that Plato accorded the virtue of justice is
found throughout his writings. Even in the *Laws* justice never loses
its preeminent position among the virtues. Not only must every
constitution, despite its imperfections, involve justice to some extent, but justice is vital in any association, good or bad. Justice, as
the civilizing virtue, makes people fit to participate in society.

The study of justice constitutes an excellent point of transition
from the study of ethics to the study of politics, inasmuch as justice
is essentially a social ethic as is Plato's political philosophy. Accordingly, we may now turn our attention to ethics on a group level, that
is, to a consideration of Plato's social ethics or political philosophy.

CHAPTER 5

Political Philosophy: The Ideal State

A T the height of his writing career and at the mature age of about forty, Plato authored what was to be acclaimed as his greatest work, the *Republic*. A masterpiece of dialogue, the *Republic* did more than explicate Plato's political philosophy, for it presented his philosophy of education as well. Even more, it contained an entire value theory together with an ethical theory. But it did not stop there, for the *Republic* contains treatises on metaphysics and psychology, a philosophy of history, and a theory of economics. The book exhibits a freshness that captivates modern readers despite its having been written about two and a half millennia ago.

Although Plato wrote two other major treatises on political philosophy, the *Statesman* and the *Laws*, neither of these reflects the belletristic talent evident in the *Republic*, nor are the ideas expressed in them on as high a level as the *Republic*. His last work on political philosophy, the *Laws*, written when he was well along in years, does not have as much exciting and effervescent dialogue as the *Republic*, written when Plato was at the peak of his writing ability.

I *The* Republic *and The* Laws: *A Comparison*

In at least two respects, however, the *Laws* went beyond the *Republic*. The principal thesis of the *Laws*, "that peace is better than war," had the effect of downgrading the virtue of courage to the lowest point on the Platonic scale of excellence. In the *Republic*, Plato, still a child of his times, recognized the important role of war. Consequently, he assigned one of the three classes of society to the business of war and included courage as a vitally important virtue, second only to wisdom. In the *Laws*, however, Plato regarded courage as merely the accidental gift of nature, a merely brutish quality

81

shared by children and animals alike. To elevate courage to a status of respectable excellence, he then defined it, when applied to human beings, as the ability to withstand insidious erotic desires and the temptations of pleasure. Regarding peace as nobler than war, Plato condemned military nations, as, for example, the Spartan state. If war became inevitable, however, then Plato would organize his moderately sized state of 5,040 citizens (and also their wives) into a military force that would astonish even the Spartans at the peak of their power. (In the *Republic* only one thousand warriors were to be enrolled.)

Aristotle concurred fully with Plato's later conclusion that the normal business of the state is peacetime activity, and that war is an anomaly. The Spartan nation, observed Aristotle, ever geared for war and not for peace, in times of peace rusted as a sword in a scabbard. Because the Spartans did not study the ways of peace, Sparta deteriorated in the absence of war. The question was whether peace or war was normal for mankind. Which was the interlude: peace or war? For Plato and Aristotle peace was the norm, but for the Spartans, war was regarded as the norm and the natural way for mankind. Aristotle asserted that the destruction of the Spartan nation must be attributed to this belief.[1]

Just as perfect health is preferable to the need to cure a disease, so peace is more desirable than victory, argued Plato, who declared that

the best is neither war nor faction . . . but peace and mutual good will. Nor is the victory of the State over itself [civil war] to be regarded as a really good thing but a necessary evil. A man might as well say that the body was in its best state when sick and cured by medicine, ignoring that there is a state of the body which needs no cure. So, if a man takes a similar view of the happiness of the city, or indeed, of the individual man—I mean, if external wars are the first and only object of his regard—he will never be a true statesman, nor will any man be a finished legislator, unless he legislates for war as a means to peace, rather than for peace as a means to war.[2]

Peace, asserted Plato, is nobler than war.

The low esteem Plato accorded to commercial pursuits in the *Republic* was considerably moderated in the *Laws*. Although reiterating the corrupting influence of commerce on people and nations by those engaged in trading (brokers, shippers, and the like rather than artisans, farmers, and other growers and producers),

Plato's attitudes and feelings concerning the matter were noticeably changed, owing to his recognition of the vital need of commerce in the interests of the state. As a means of reforming this segment of society, Plato toyed with the idea of having some of the finest citizens enter the commercial world in order that it might acquire a better image. In the *Laws*, he expressed his discontent with the military-industrial complex and its detrimental effect on the nation.

Plato rose above his time in still a third respect in writing the *Laws*. Whereas in his earlier writings Plato dwelt on the theme of homosexuality as if it were normal, and despite his description of it in the words of Socrates and others, he repudiated it as unnatural in the *Laws*. "I think that the pleasure is to be deemed natural which arises out of the intercourse between men and women," declared Plato, "but that the intercourse of men with men, or of women with women, is contrary to nature, and that the bold attempt was originally due to unbridled lust."[3] Plato held that leisure time was a serious impediment to wholesome living, for it prompted salaciousness, licentiousness, and lasciviousness. He cited the sexual behavior of animals as evidence of the unnaturalness of homosexuality. He held "it wrong that male should have to do carnally with youthful male as with female," and "from evidence from the life of the animals . . . male does not touch male in this way because the action is unnatural."[4] He considered incestuousness infamy.

Another comparison between the *Republic* and the *Laws* indicates that while one depicts the best of all states—thus painting a picture of an ideal republic—the other provides us with the second-best or the most practical one under prevailing circumstances. The *Republic* emphasizes the principle that justice and right will be achieved through the rule or leadership of the philosopher-king, whereas the *Laws* takes into consideration the need for practicality and expediency and is designed to guide the benevolent dictator, even if he is a tyrant or despot. The *Republic* espouses an aristocracy, but the *Laws* favors an oligarchal democracy or, in the terminology of Plato's most distinguished pupil, Aristotle, a polity. Aristotle's *Politics* considers Plato's "whole system of government . . . to be neither democracy nor oligarchy, but something in a mean between them, which is usually called a polity, and is composed of heavy-armed soldiers."[5] While Plato's ideal state was a republic with its accompanying constitution, the *Laws*, as the title indicates, endowed the ideal state with laws but no constitution.

Actually, in the *Laws* there is little mention of a constitution. But both dialogues are quite specific respecting their favored form of government. The ideal state of the *Republic* called for an aristocracy, portraying democracy and tyranny as defective or corruptive types of a good form of government. The *Laws*, however, calls for a synthesis of these two inferior forms of government as the preferred solution. Plato, reasoning that combining the best aspects of the two forms would be most desirable, united the freedom provided by a democratic government with the unity or harmony provided by a dictatorship. Stating the proper objectives of government in the *Laws*, Plato held that "a legislator should have three aims in his enactments—the society for which he makes them must have freedom, must have amity with itself, must have understanding."[6] He added, "With a view to this we selected two kinds of government, the most autocratic and the freest; and now we are considering which of them is the right form. We found that when we had a certain due proportionality in either case, in the one of authority, in the other of liberty, there was a maximum of well-being."[7] But when either of these forms of government is carried to an extreme, disastrous results ensue: in the case of democracy it is license and in the despotic state it is slavery.

Plato's *Republic* and *Laws* permit still another contrast. While the former gave the highest priority to the advancement of knowledge, the latter considered the molding of character to be most important. At no time, however, does Plato abandon his earlier contention that justice is based on knowledge—that one must know what is right in order to do it, and that, therefore, in order to be just one must know what justice is. But the moral tone of the *Laws* is unmistakable; centuries before the Christian era, this dialogue formulated a Platonic version of the Golden Rule and included a moral situation that anticipates the one discussed by Jesus in the Parable of the Good Samaritan.

The *Republic* advocates communism as the ideal mode of living for guardians, the ruling class. In the *Laws*, however, Plato, although portraying communistic society as the best, admitted that such an ideal society is impractical for imperfect human beings, fit only for a nation of gods, and that private ownership is the only alternative.

The *Republic* and the *Laws* discuss the problem of interest payments on loans. Plato lamented the fact that people are reduced to poverty because of inability to repay indebtedness, a situation which may cause unrest, sow the seeds of revolution, and result in class warfare leading to the downfall of the established government. In the *Republic*, he recommends merely that loans be made at the risk of the lender, but in the *Laws*, he calls for a law to the effect that "no one shall deposit money with another whom he does not trust as a friend, nor shall he lend money at interest; and the borrower should be under no obligation to repay either capital or interest."[8] It should be noted that Jesus shares Plato's view on the issue.

II *The* Republic *and the* Statesman *Contrasted*

Plato's third political treatise, the *Statesman*, differs markedly from the *Republic*, especially in expressing his loss of confidence in law and the constitution. Abandoning the idea that a nation should be ruled strictly in accordance with laws, as in the case of the philosopher-king of the *Republic*, Plato now recommends the rule of a wise man who is a law unto himself. "The best thing of all," declares Plato, "is not that the law should rule, but that a man should rule, supposing him to have wisdom and royal power."[9] This altered view can be traced to Plato's conviction that "law can never issue an injunction binding on all which really embodies what is best for each; it cannot prescribe with perfect accuracy what is good and right for each member of the community at any one time."[10] The superiority of the rule of a wise man over the rule of law is based on the fact that the law cannot cope with a diversity of particular circumstances and at best deals with generalities. Consequently, people are treated unjustly by a law, just as they are similarly mistreated by an ignorant, obstinate tyrant. According to Plato:

Law can never issue an injunction binding on all which really embodies what is best for each; it cannot prescribe with perfect accuracy what is good and right for each member of the community at any one time. The differences of human personality, the variety of men's activities, and the inevitable unsettlement attending all human experience make it impossible for any art whatsoever to issue unqualified rules holding good on all questions at all times. . . .

But we find practically always that the law tends to issue just this invariable kind of rule. It is like a self-willed, ignorant man who lets no one do anything but what he has ordered and forbids all subsequent questioning of his orders even if the situation has shown some marked improvement on the one for which he originally legislated.[11]

Since people are never uniform and constant, laws pertaining to them prove unsatisfactory. While law is not an ideal form of maintaining control, it does serve its purpose as an adjunct to the ruler. The law is analogous to the written instructions of a physician during his absence, instructions which are no longer required when he returns and devotes personal attention to his patient.

Accordingly, the best government is one free from law and under the direction of the statesman, who, unlike inflexible law, is sufficiently agile to cope with each individual case as it emerges. As an art, statesmanship can be compared with painting. Just as a work of art is not the mere product of mixing colors by following a formula, so a good state is not the result of laws. Government is best, then, when independent of law. In the absence of an outstanding and true statesman, however, a government under law is preferred to governments without law. Only a true statesman can unite citizens to form a lasting society. The best government, then, is government by one scientific ruler, that is, "government by a real statesman using real statecraft,"[12] namely, political science.

In addition to this best type of government by a statesman, Plato discusses six inferior forms of government. These alternative types of government may have to be considered if no true statesman is available to govern. The six divide into three couplets: (a) the government by one: (1) monarchy and (2) tyranny; (b) government by the few: (3) aristocracy and (4) oligarchy; and (c) government by the many: (5) constitutional democracy (duly constituted government which rules the people under law so as to implement their constitution) and (6) anarchic democracy (mob rule without recourse to any law or constitution).

Because power has been diffused into the entire citizenry and has consequently been diluted, democracy is the weakest form of government, hence it is impotent in doing very much good—or evil. Monarchy is the most efficient of these half-dozen defective forms of government owing to its concentration of power in a single person. When there is no ideal person available to be the king (president), regulation of the monarchy by law is necessary. Nevertheless, monarchy is the most efficient and therefore the best of the six alternative types of government. In the absence of restraint, however, monarchy degenerates into tyranny, becoming the bitterest form of oppression under which to live. An aristocracy is not as good as a monarchy, but better than a democracy because, although aristocracy lacks the efficiency of monarchy, it is more effective than a democracy. Of the two forms of government by the few, aristocracy is regarded as superior to oligarchy. The rule of law breaks down both in tyranny and in an oligarchy, but the latter is a less oppressive regime. Because power is distributed among relatively few people, oligarchies in states which do not observe the rule of law are not as bad as tyrannies, but not as good as democracies. The inefficiency of a democracy shows up badly in law-abiding countries, but in lawless ones this very inefficiency is their very salvation. Consequently in countries where law is flouted, a democracy is preferred to an oligarchy or tyranny. Where lawlessness reigns, a despot can do greater evil than an oligarchic or democratic government. In a nation without a constitution, democracy is preferred to oligarchy because democracy can do less evil.

Thus it is necessary to assess the good and evil results of diverse forms of government, as in choosing between constitutional government for law-abiding citizens and governments which obey no laws. The three lawful types are in descending order of efficiency, monarchy, aristocracy, and democracy. In a monarchy, one person rules under law; in an aristocracy, a few persons rule in accordance with the provisions of a constitution; and in a democracy, the sovereignty belongs to all the people but the rulers must abide by the laws.

Corresponding to these three forms of government under law are three lawless types: tyranny (autocratic rule by one person) oligarchy (despotic rule by the privileged few); and democracy (mob rule, and anarchic or lawless condition). Since Plato could find no descriptive terms to distinguish democracy under law from democracy without law, he used the single term "democracy" for both types. Aristotle referred to them as constitutional democracies and democracies without a polity. (All seven forms of government described by Plato are shown in the accompanying schematic diagram).

Aristotle evaluated six of the seven forms of government discussed by Plato. He regarded as good forms of government all three (monarchy, aristocracy, and polity) in which the rulers govern with due consideration for the welfare of the citizens. If the rulers sacrifice the public interest for the sake of private gain, a corrupt form of government emerges. Monarchy degenerates into tyranny, aristocracy into oligarchy, and polity into democracy. Thus, in Aristotle's view, any government, whether there be one, a few, or many

Plato's Seven Forms of Government as Found in His *Republic*

Order of Preference

(A) One Perfect Form

Statesman

(B) Only Available Forms of Government Remaining

I. Countries with Respect for Law — II. Countries Where the Law is Flouted

(a) Rule of one

1. Monarchy   2. Tyranny

(b) Rule of the few

3. Aristocracy   4. Oligarchy

(c) Rule of many

5. Democracy (with a constitution)   6. Democracy (without constitutional law)

Order of Preference

rulers, can be either good or corrupt, depending upon its motivation and aims.

Both Plato and Aristotle denigrate democracy. After all, it was a democracy that put Socrates to death. "Democracy," declared Plato sarcastically, "is a charming form of government, anarchic and motley, assigning a kind of equality indiscriminately to equals and unequals alike."[13]

Aristotle fused two good forms of government together, namely, government by a truly statesmanlike ruler and government by a king. Plato had separated the two, elevating the former to a class by itself as the perfect form of government. For Plato, the best government is the seventh type, that of the true statesman who applies to the solution of governmental problems his knowledge of political science and statecraft. Hence he ascribes to knowledge the highest importance, a point of view he derived originally from the teachings of Socrates who insisted that any person who knows what is right will do it.

Plato discusses the qualities of personality most desirable for a ruler to possess. He considers two types, the courageous or aggressive and the gentle or temperate personalities, and concludes that either of these conflicting temperaments is deplorable if carried to an extreme. These qualities should complement each other in the same leader so that the end result will be a moderate disposition and a well–balanced state program of government. An over-aggressive ruler precipitates unnecessary conflicts and wars, whereas one who is too timid makes the state an easy prey for its enemies to conquer.

According to Plato

There is no difficulty in forging these human bonds if the divine bond has been forged first. That bond is a conviction about values and standards shared by both types of character. For indeed the whole business of kingly weaving is comprised in this and this alone,—in never allowing the self-restrained personalities to be separated from the courageous; to avoid this he must make the fabric close and firm by working common beliefs in the hearts of each type of citizen and making public honors and triumphs subserve this end, and finally, each must be involved with the other in the solemn pledges of matrimony. When he has woven his web smooth and close, . . . he must entrust the various offices of state to them to be shared.[14]

When a state function calls for the appointment of one person, the statesman should select an individual in whom both qualities (gentleness and courage) are combined, but if the appointment calls for several employees, he should choose some from each type of personality so that they can work together as a unified team.

Aristotle did not agree with Plato that the law is only a general rule which the statesman should be free to modify in accordance with changing circumstances, for such a policy would allow arbitrary decisions to be made on crucial matters. The idea of selecting the best and giving him a status above the law was repugnant to Aristotle, who held that "no one is immeasurably superior to others as to represent adequately the greatness and dignity of the office."[15]

III   Plato's Republic: *The Ideal State*

In the *Republic*, Plato discusses the problem of injustice. Its solution—the way to achieve social justice and happiness—provides the principal theme of the treatise. It is only when this issue is resolved that the question of the nature and character of the good state, an ideal state, can be determined. Justice in a person or state is an indication of health. The just, who are healthier than the unjust, are by virtue of that fact also happier. Thus, in presenting his political philosophy, Plato was at the same time developing a "science" of ethics.

Plato's thoughts are, accordingly, concerned with the good individual and the good state. He assumed what every Greek considered obvious, namely, that in order to be a good person, one must participate in and be an active part of the state. Anyone who chooses to be a "man without a country" thereby diminishes himself as a human being; or, as Aristotle, Plato's celebrated student, was later to declare: "Man is by nature a political animal."[16]

Emerging as of paramount importance are questions concerning the nature and structure of the good state as well as the qualities which make a person good. The influence of Socrates is seen in Plato's statement that knowledge is the precondition to goodness, for did not Socrates proclaim that he who knows what is good will *ipso facto* do what is good? In his discussion of education Plato considers what knowledge is required in order to insure a good state—in other words, the proper training of citizens.

Distinctive features of Plato's political philosophy distinguishing it from others of his time include his advocacy of rule by selected philosophers on the basis of merit, the practice of communism among members of the guardian class, and an improved status for women—features highlighted in the *Republic* and the *Laws* so as to give his views a modern liberal flavor. Certainly his proposal for the emancipation of women, so that they would no longer be confined to their homes but would be educated and assume their roles as active participants in government equally with men, must have struck a discordant note among his contemporaries; that was a most unusual idea, a much more radical notion than his theory in favor of communism.

Plato's proposed system of "communism," which required common ownership of all property, had precedents in both Sparta and Crete. Aristotle reported that some communistic practices "prevail at Sparta and Crete respecting common meals, whereby the legislator has made property common."[17] According to Aristotle, the community of wives in Plato's *Republic* reminded him of the licentiousness of Spartan women, where "husband and wife being each a part of every family . . . . live in every sort of intemperance."[18] He noted also that Spartan women, equally with men, were put in charge of many important tasks of the community.

IV *The Founding of the Ideal State*

Plato appears to have been the first philosopher to formulate a "social contract" theory of government. In the *Republic*, Glaucon argues that the state and its institutions owe their origins to the tacit consent of the citizens, because they are mere conventions made by humans and can therefore be altered or abolished by the people who created them. Thus the state is but a social compact. Explaining the origin of the state, Glaucon declares: "When men have wronged and been wronged by one another, and have the taste of the two in their mouths, those who are without the power to do wrong or to keep from being wronged make a social compact with one another to put an end to both. And this is the start, they say, of ordered society, of law-making, and of agreements between men [justice]."[19]

Plato, however, who did not agree with Glaucon's explanation contended that political societies arise as a natural result of efforts to meet the needs of human beings. "A State," Plato wrote, "arises, as I conceive, out of the needs of mankind; no one is self-sufficing, but all of us have many wants."[20]

Social Class Stratification: the Artisans. Reiterating that basic needs of people are the primary factor in the creation of a state, Plato goes on to delineate those needs as food, shelter, clothing, and the like. To meet these physical needs requires that the first citizens in a state should be farmers, builders, weavers or makers of clothes, shoemakers, and other craftsmen contributing essential physical goods and services. He maintains that less than a half-dozen workers are needed in order to establish the most primitive kind of society. Each type of worker, however, must not attempt to meet only his own needs but cater to all other citizens so that, for example, the shoemaker provides shoes for the entire community.

The result is that each member of the society acquires an expertise of his own that is shared for the benefit of all. In this way not only is more produced but the quality is excellent because each person concentrates upon his specialty. The consequence is a community of experts. Thus, a farmer will not be slowed in his work because he has made an imperfect tool, such as a plough. An expert craftsman will construct a superior tool for him.

Imports will be necessary to obtain useful goods not produced within the state; and surplus domestic goods will have to be exported. Therefore merchants, shippers, shipowners, sailors, and others experienced in foreign trade will be required, in addition to an acceptable currency and a marketplace where shops, shopkeepers, and hired help will be available.

When basic physical needs have been provided for by establishing a division of labor (in terms of each person's natural ability or aptitude), the lowest rung on the ladder leading to a civilized state has been reached. As a consequence, justice in an economic sense has been realized. "Tell me whether I am right or not," remarked Plato. "You remember the original principle we were always laying down at the foundation of the state, that one man should practice one thing only, the thing to which his nature was best adapted;— Well, I believe that principle, or some form of it, is justice."[21] This notion of justice as the "minding of one's own business" is valid provided that each worker is truly fit to perform his assigned task. Injustice and the unhappiness it causes must be attributed to society's misfits, people whose occupations run counter to their natures, dispositions, abilities, and aptitudes. Not only does unfitness for a task prove disruptive to the state, but the worker himself is frustrated and thereby made unhappy. For a person to be content he must not assume jobs for which he is ill-suited. To do so will result in defective workmanship, a maladjusted personality, and a person who is perpetually discontent.

The farmers, craftsmen, traders, and exporters, the lowest group in the Platonic social order, constitute the class of artisans. Their needs seem to be readily satisfied through accumulation of material goods and satisfaction of their sensual appetites. Their highest objective in life is gain, that is, the acquisition of material wealth; they value other things only insofar as such things contribute to this one end. Their education is quite limited, consisting of the same early education provided for the two other Platonic classes of citizens, but nothing beyond the primary level.

Plato held that the primitive type of state tends to develop in the direction of luxury, acquiring certain refinements but becoming subject to unwholesome and detrimental influences. As the state moves away from the simple life described above, its people cultivate a desire for luxury foods, for entertainment made available by actors, dancers, female singers, musicians, poets, painters, and other artists. To fulfill the increased demand of the people for luxuries, the nation must expand by moving into the territory of another nation. "The country which was enough to support the original inhabitants," observed Plato, "will be too small now, and not enough." What happens then? "Then a slice of our neighbors' land will be wanted by us for pasture and tillage, and they will want a slice of ours, if, like ourselves, they exceed the limits of necessity, and give themselves up to the unlimited accumulation of wealth."[22]

Thus, according to Plato, the lust for luxury is at the root of war. To cope with these unwholesome developments, the state must once again enlarge its domain. It organizes an entire army to defend itself and to satisfy the greed of its citizens. Inasmuch as the ideal state calls for each task to be performed by the person best qualified, by an expert, a citizen army simply will not do. Warriors, fitted for the task by nature, armed with courage and skills developed through a lifetime of training and drilling, are selected as the specialists who will practice the art of warfare. Plato called them warrior guardians.

The Auxiliary Class: The Warriors. A defenseless nation cannot long withstand threats to its survival either from hostile nations or from enemies within. The vital business of war must not be entrusted to amateurs. Consequently, a class of courageous military recruits who have acquired expertise, must undertake the task of defending the state.

Like the class of artisans, the warriors, in addition to being properly schooled in the art of warfare, must possess a native aptitude suited to this calling. Whereas the excellence displayed by the artisan class of citizens is self-control (appetitive control), the virtue distinguishing the military is courage. Aggression, the cause of war, is the characteristic trait of the warriors. As the desire of the people for luxury increases, the aggressive personality emerges. Only if the people give up their excessive desire for luxury will they be able to diminish the spread of aggression.

The personality of the warrior class is characterized by fierceness, pugnacity, aggressiveness, fearlessness, indomitability, and anger. They possess an excellence or virtue, courage, and they are motivated, not by any intense desire for profit or wealth, as is the case with the artisans, but only by considerations of honorable conduct. Spurred on by the ambition to serve the nation, they stand ready to die for the reward of being revered and remembered on the rolls of honor. Like spirited horses that require bridling, however, the spirited warriors must be tamed. These warrior guardians must be controlled by a superior class of guardians, the philosopher-rulers, who are motivated by a love of wisdom.

The auxiliary guardian class must perform three important functions: (1) do the fighting, (2) enforce domestic laws, and (3) carry out the orders of the guardian class of rulers. It is therefore imperative not only that they be well-trained and educated for their responsible tasks but also that their appetite for greed and gain be curbed. To achieve this end they must be humanized through education. Otherwise, instead of protecting their charges, they might turn against those whom they should be guarding.

Care must be exercised to see that the auxiliaries or guards do not raid the citizens like savage tyrants simply because they are stronger. Effective education, training, and control over their style of life will be required. Spartan simplicity and discipline must dominate their lives. Basic necessities of life befitting victors must be provided for them. They should be quartered in houses suitable for men of war rather than men of property, but comfortable enough so that they will not be tempted to blame and mistreat their fellow citizens. They must not be allowed to own their houses or other private property except the barest necessaries. Their diet must be planned to meet the needs of warriors in training. They will be garrisoned together and share their meals in common. Their wages should be fixed at the minimum level required for bare living expenses in order to avoid the corrupting influence of money. Frugality will save them from arrogance and preserve the commonwealth. Should any of them aspire to become landed gentry, they will forfeit their status as guardians, lowering themselves to the level of farmers and merchants and thereby incurring the emnity of their fellow citizens. Such men, instead of being respected, will spend their lives in an atmosphere of hostility, hating and being hated. For the auxiliaries alone among the entire population, said Plato:

it is unlawful to touch or handle gold or silver; they must not be under the same roof with it, or wear any, or drink from gold or silver goblets; in this way they may preserve themselves and the city. If they themselves acquire private land and houses and currency, they will be household managers and farmers instead of guardians, hostile masters of the other citizens instead of their allies; they will spend their whole life hating and being hated, plotting and being plotted against; they will pass their entire life in much greater terror of internal than of external enemies, and they will hasten themselves and the rest of the state to virtual ruin.[23]

Notwithstanding the severe living conditions of this lower guardian group, the auxiliaries, it would not surprise Plato if the warrior-guardians were quite happy with their lot in life. But Plato emphasizes the fact that in planning his ideal state, it is not his intention to insure the happiness of any one segment of society; rather, the aim is to achieve happiness for the state as a whole. "Our guardians may very likely be the happiest of men," he declared, but "our aim in founding the State was not the disproportionate happiness of any one class, but the greatest happiness of the whole; we thought that in a State which is ordered with a view to the good of the whole we should be most likely to find justice, and in the ill-ordered State injustice."[24] Happiness, said Plato, is the result of justice; the unhappy state is deficient in justice. When the people in any state become expert in their respective crafts, they will find as much happiness as is possible for them within the limits imposed by their natural capacities and environment. In fact, since the warrior-guardians are free from the burdens imposed upon other classes— rearing and caring for a family, concern about money, and other evils—they will be a blessed lot. "From all these evils," Plato asserted, "they will be delivered, and they will live a happier life than that men count most happy, the life of the victors at Olympia."[25] Is theirs not preferable to the life of craftsmen, merchants, and artisans?

The Ruling Class: The Guardians. In his *Republic*, Plato had originally put the warriors and the guardian rulers into a single class, inasmuch as warriors were to serve as military guardians of the state, cooperating with the rulers. There were thus two levels of guardians, a lower level of warriors to defend the state, and a higher level of rulers to govern the state. At a later stage of the *Republic*, Plato drew sharper distinctions, describing the guardians as the superior ruling class, and relegating the warriors to a subordinate status as auxiliaries.

Accordingly, Plato now had three distinct classes: (1) the guardians or rulers who make up the deliberative or legislative body of the state; (2) the auxiliaries or warriors, including both the administrative (or executive) personnel and the military forces of the nation; and (3) the artisans or craftsmen, the productive members of society. This classification made it clear that the auxiliaries, the lower level of guardians, are subject to the authority of the higher level of guardians who serve as rulers of the state.

Plato's republic is not a social or hereditary aristocracy in which each person is born into a caste system, owing to his ancestry, but an aristocracy based upon personal qualifications. The individual's natural talents or aptitudes determine his class rank. Consequently, a child born to a member of one class can be shifted to a higher or lower class because of his special capacities and excellences. Thus there is a democratic element in Plato's ideal state, permitting each person an equal opportunity to attain even the highest positions, including that of head of the state. Everyone has an equal chance to become president of the republic. For any high post, however, the applicant must prove that he is worthy and qualified, especially that he has governed himself well by resisting temptation and successfully coping with life's challenges and vicissitudes. "If we find one bearing himself well in all these trials and resisting every enchantment, a true guardian of himself, preserving always that perfect rhythm and harmony of being which he has acquired from his training," observed Plato, "such a one will be of the greatest service to the commonwealth as well as to himself. Whenever we find one who has come unscathed through every test in childhood, youth, and manhood, we shall set him as a ruler to watch over the commonwealth."[26]

A true guardian makes the country's concern and welfare the guiding rule of his life. "Guardian in the fullest sense," asserted Plato, "ought to be applied only to this higher class who preserve us against foreign enemies and maintain peace among our citizens at home, so that neither enemies without shall have the power, nor their friends within the desire to harm the city. The young men whom we before called guardians may be more properly designated auxiliaries who will enforce the decisions of the rulers."[27]

The guardians must see to it that while noble qualities of humanity emerge and become dominant among the people, the unworthy or evil qualities decline. For this reason the rulers must carefully guard the purity of the race, permitting only the most suitable amalgamations or admixtures of parentage in order to produce the best possible progeny. Rulers, said Plato,

should observe what elements mingle in their offspring; for if the son of a golden or silver parent has an admixture of brass and iron, then nature orders a transposition of ranks, and the eye of the ruler must not be pitiful towards the child because he has to descend in the scale and become a farmer or workman, just as there may be sons of artisans who having an admixture of gold or silver in them are raised to honor, and become guardians or auxiliaries."[28]

Merit, then, rather than hereditary birth, fits one for membership in the governing class.

Wealth and poverty, those twin evils, must be expunged from the state, for the former fosters indolence, and the latter gives birth to meanness and viciousness. Both are responsible for discontent among the people. A craftsman on becoming wealthy, for example, will allow the quality of his work to deteriorate; and the poverty-stricken artisan will not be able to afford the wherewithal to carry on his craft with excellence. Wealth and poverty are equally subversive of the interests of the state, and it is the responsibility of the guardians to prevent either extreme from arising in the state.

The auxiliaries need only to know what is right to believe and do, knowledge which they receive from the rulers, the guardians. But the latter, in order to execute their duties competently, must possess wisdom so that their counsel will be good and prudent. The guardians must possess insight into what is good so that they will know what is good for the state as a whole. It is, then, the love of wisdom, the philosophic spirit, that characterizes the ability to rule. Consequently, the head of state must be a philosopher. "Until philosophers become kings," declared Plato, "or kings and rulers of this world devote themselves to the pursuit of philosophy seriously and adequately, until political power and philosophical intelligence coalesce, and the motley horde of natures who now pursue the one to the exclusion of the other are compelled from doing so, neither our states nor the human race will have respite from evil."[29]

While the mark of a philosopher is his love of wisdom and the possession of wisdom is his excellence, the virtue characterizing the fighting force of warrior-guardians is courage. But courage, devoid of knowledge is not a virtue. The courage displayed by an animal, for example, is not a virtue. For courage to qualify as a virtue, a person must be cognizant of what truly should or should not elicit fear. Being brave will mean, then, being aware of the kinds of things which it is proper to fear, an awareness which must be derived through education provided by the philosopher-guardians. "Right conviction about the things which ought or ought not to be feared is what I call courage,"[30] said Plato.

Of the three classes, the craftsmen, the fighting force, and the guardian rulers, the smallest in number is the ruling class, the next in order are the auxiliaries; and by far the largest number are the great multitudes of artisans.

Plato reiterates that, in addition to wisdom, the rulers must possess both courage and temperance. Temperance, defined as self-mastery, is a condition in which the higher self, the reason, dominates the lower self, the spirited and concupiscent impulses. Temperance means harmony in one's personality, the absence of emotional conflict, a kind of orderliness, a control of certain pleasure and appetites, enabling one to be "master of oneself." A person is "his own master when the part which is better by nature has the worse under its control."[31] Conversely, intemperance means the reverse process, whereby a person is "a slave to himself."

It is up to the ruling class of philosophers, who have attained the virtues themselves, to instill them into the multitude of society as well as in the characters of individuals in subordinate classes. The elite, therefore, with their superior education and inborn dispositions, can accomplish this task owing to their own self-restraint and wisdom. When "the desires of the inferior many are controlled by the desires and the knowledge of the fewer and better," held Plato, then "if any society can be called master of itself and in control of its pleasures and desires, it will be ours."[32]

In this way the people will be unified in their beliefs and desires, and harmony will prevail between the ruling and governed classes. Since the people share the same beliefs they will readily agree upon the choice of rulers. The populace obeys by consent, and the government rules with the consent of those governed, a principle of freedom clearly elaborated in the *Republic*. Democratic freedom, however, in the sense of licentiousness or a "free for all" society is repudiated.

Like personal temperance, social temperance, that is, the practice of moderation by individuals in their relationship to the state, is necessary. "This unanimity would rightly be called moderation, harmonious agreement between the naturally superior and inferior elements as to which of the two should rule, whether with respect to the state or in the individual."[33] Justice dictates that this arrangement be recognized and accepted, since by nature men are endowed with specific aptitudes that fit them for certain occupations suited to their natures. To flout our natures is to frustrate our true selves, become misfits, and create our own unhappiness as well as contribute to the prevalence of injustice. Although it is merely an error for the cobbler and carpenter to exchange jobs, an interchange of careers between fighting men and philosopher-rulers would prove disastrous not only to the individual himself, but also to society as a whole. "Suppose," said Plato, "that someone who is by nature an artisan or tradesman gets so above himself—through wealth, influence, or physical might—as to push himself into the class of fighting men, or one of the soldiers should aspire beyond his merits into the class of legislators and guardians, and either to assume the duties or implements of the other; or when one man functions as trader, legislator, and warrior all in one, then I think you will agree with me in saying that this kind of exchange and meddling is the ruin of the State."[34] Justice, then, is a feature of that society in which each member functions in the capacity dictated by his natural aptitude and disposition. When the three principal agencies (deliberative, executive, and productive) are manned by appropriate personnel performing their respective tasks, justice prevails, for it is then that ideal justice shines through with its attendant happiness. On the one hand, the state is a reflection of its constituent members, while on the other hand, the citizens reflect the qualities dominating their society, Consequently, the qualities of the nation—deliberative (wisdom), auxiliary (courage), and productive (self-control)—will be found in each individual in the society, although different degrees of development will be manifest because each type of individual enters life differing in potential capacity, and each can be educated only to the extent that his innate aptitude permits. For Plato, virtue means ability or excellence. Among the producers within a society—the productive class—excellence requires self-control displayed in the form of obedience to the laws and the ruling class. Self-control is of course a virtue needed by all classes of society, but it is imperative and primary for the guardians of the republic, who must practice self-mastery in order to perform their duties.

V *Communal Life and the Equality of Women*

Plato prescribed communism for only one class, the guardian rulers, who must share all things in common, including wives, children, and property. The purpose of this arrangement was to eliminate the causes of political corruption. A statesman without a family will not be susceptible to nepotism, nor will he be open to bribery, since he is not allowed to possess any kind of property, including monetary wealth. Instead of residing in private homes with their individual families, the guardians live in a commune as a single family. Consequently, any temptation to devote their interest, time, and wealth to the family rather than the state will be resisted.

Sexual intercourse is restricted to class members only; that is, male guardians can have sexual relations only with female members of the guardian class. This rule, designed for eugenic reasons, is intended to insure that the finest possible breed of children will be available to serve the best interests of the state; but the rule does not mean, however, that the children of the guardians automatically become permanent members of the guardian class, for they will be relegated to a lower class if their natural talents or aptitudes are insufficient to justify membership in the class of guardians. Members of a lower class will rise to the guardian class if blessed with sufficient natural aptitude. Furthermore, Plato's intention was not to license promiscuity among the guardian class but to control it, inasmuch as promiscuity would subvert the eugenic objectives to an even greater degree than the current practice of choosing one's own partner freely.

Other radical departures from the culture of his time include Plato's recommendation that the guardian class of women should live in close association with men, dine at common tables with them, and exercise together (despite their nakedness) in the gymnasiums. If this experience aroused them sexually, then all the better, for Plato wanted the guardian men to be attracted to the women of their class. "The guardians of either sex should have all their pursuits in common," and "the wives of our guardians are to be common, and their children are to be common, and no parent is to know his own child, nor any child his parent."[35] Furthermore, the guardian women "must be as far as possible of like natures with them; and they must live in common houses and meet at common meals. None of them will have anything specially his or her own; they will be together, and will be brought up together, and will associate at gymnastic exercises. And so they will be drawn by a necessity of their natures to have intercourse with each other."[36]

Women of the guardian class will also share the same education as their male counterparts. Inasmuch as the two sexes share the same original nature, it follows that whatever education is beneficial for one will prove of equal worth to the other; that is, whatever makes a man a good guardian will also make a woman a good guardian. Since men and women share the same qualities, the two sexes should follow the same careers, including service as rulers of the state as well as defenders of the nation in time of war. Plato's was an across the board equality. "Must we not assign the same pursuits to the same natures?" he inquired rhetorically. He pointed out that any "woman may have a guardian nature," and added, "With a view to having women guardians, we should not have one kind of education to fashion the men, and another for the women, especially as they have the same nature to begin with."[37] Consequently, "the women then must strip for their physical training, since they will be clothed in excellence. They must share in war and the other duties of the guardians about the city."[38] One distinction between the sexes drawn by Plato was that the women, being somewhat weaker physically, will not be assigned physically strenuous responsibilities. Guardian females working in the *ecclesia* ("congress" or "parliament") need not be concerned for the welfare of their offspring during their absence, inasmuch as nurses will tend them. The children are removed from their mothers for the same reason that fathers are not permitted to know which of the children they sired, namely, to prevent nepotism, favoritism, and the like. Nursing mothers are ignorant as to whether or not it is their own child that is being suckled by them.

A second distinction between the sexes made by Plato was the difference in the prime of life for each. While twenty to forty years of age was a woman's prime of life, the age was twenty to fifty-five years for a man. These were to be the age limits for begetting children. Guardians of distinction, especially young heroes, were to mate more frequently than the average. Plato was not suggesting polygamy, which would allow the men to have sex with a different woman in sequence, but only that the men be permitted more frequent sexual contacts during periodic marriage festivals. Cohabitation of couples was practiced during festival periods, lasting about a month. At the close of the marriage festival, partnerships or marriages were dissolved, with the participants remaining celibate during the interim between marriage festivals. Plato vaguely hints at infanticide as a way of disposing of defective children, a Spartan custom, but actually proposes that inferior offspring of guardians should be adopted and cared for by the class of artisans.

VI   Five Forms of Government and Their Accompanying Personality Types

Although Plato cited five types of government in the *Republic*, he regarded only one of them, the monarchy, as the good form, the others (timocracy, oligarchy, democracy, and tyranny) as inferior or defective forms. Plato's monarchy was not a hereditary royalty, nor did it necessarily mean life tenure. The ruler must be of middle age and have had many years of intellectual training and have passed through a successful apprenticeship in the tasks of government. Theoretical knowledge and a record of successful practice are prerequisites.

There is only one way in which heredity plays a part in the selection of the philosopher-king who, for Plato, is the only legitimate reigning monarch, since only he rules with the consent of the people. The philosopher-king, owing to the fortunate arrangement of his genes, is endowed by nature with necessary aptitude for royal training and education. Any person, male or female, who displays incisive intellect, courageous spirit, and self-mastery must be credited with royal qualities and personality. Add to these qualities a successful education and practical experience in the political arena and you will have the nearly qualified candidate. Nearly qualified candidate, we say, because a fully adequate candidate for the position of philosopher-king must have acquired the cardinal Platonic virtues and have dialectical knowledge of the Good. Are these requirements excessive? They are hardly that, Plato argues, if one considers the fact that the entire welfare of a country, of all its citizens, is in the hands of a single ruler.

The Government as the Reflection of the Personality of Its Citizens. A discerning citizen who rightly condemns the character and conduct of leaders in government should assign most of the blame to the citizens, because the government is merely a reflection of the people, and they have acquired the same characteristics as their government. A state is just if its citizens are just; a corrupt state mirrors precisely the evil dispositions of those governed.

Plato's ideal state is one in which justice rules both within the personality of the philosopher-king and throughout the nation. Justice prevails in both because the rule of the intellect dominates in both. After all, Plato asks, does not the person who knows what is right automatically proceed toward effecting it? It is he who basks in the joy of wisdom, freedom, and justice.

To the extent that the government deviates from the qualities of the ideal state and the character of its philosopher-king, to that same extent the nation deteriorates. Plato cited four steps of increasing regression from the ideal rule of the philosopher-king, that is to say, from the ideal of a monarchy or an aristocracy ruled by one person; these steps in descending order of regression are timocracy, oligarchy, democracy, and tyranny. Thus, when the ideal state, the monarchy of the philosopher-king, falls, timocracy emerges; with the fall of timocracy, oligarchy arises; that failing, democracy appears; the demise of democracy spells anarchy and the rise of tyranny.

The Ideal State's Demise: The Development of the Timocratic Personality and Timarchy. Realizing that nothing in the temporal world is everlasting, Plato knew that even if his ideal state of philosopher-kings ever did come into existence, it, like all things temporal, would pass away. Its passing would signal the rise of a new type of personality pervading the nation, the timocratic individual. Prizing honor, and courage as the excellence whence all honor generates, the timocratic personality, motivated by the ambitious craving for honor *(timē)*, is ever desirous of having the country ruled by those to whom honor should be accorded. In other words, driven by their admiration for courage, these timocrats honor those they admire by offering them the chief positions of government.

Plato considered the displacement of aristocracy, the rule of the philosopher-king, by timocracy to be a perversion or miscarriage of justice. Platonic justice, by definition, requires each person to assume his rightful role and task in society. By this definition, timocrats should not be rulers but members of the military forces defending the nation. They do not belong in the legislative branch. The reason Plato considered timocracy a perversion is that it displaced the rule of wisdom, and thus prostituted wisdom to honor, that is to say, the spirited aggressive aspect of the self has usurped the role of the rational aspect. Hence, reason is cast aside to permit the domination of the self by ambition. The same holds true in society when lust for honor, rather than for the enlightenment of reason, holds sway and directs the course that the nation will follow. Rather than thinking one's way through issues, individuals and the nation emote their way through problems. It is as if the heart coerced the head to do its bidding rather than the head enlightening the heart.

Plato cited Sparta and Crete as timocratic forms of government. Their elevated passions of avarice and ambition, compounded with their distrust of the intellect, resulted in criminality and in Sparta the virtual destruction of the nation. They esteemed only courage, the virtue of the soldier, but for a nation to prevail it must excel in the virtues of peace: self-mastery or moderation, wisdom, and justice. Should a wave of the timocratic personality overtake the nation, so that its auxiliaries become avaricious, then such widespread greed would allow the military to snatch the ruling power from the ideal guardians, the philosophical rulers.

Civil strife, said Plato, is the catalyst active in the downfall of governments. He felt that civil enmity and war are generated out of disharmony, diversity, and injustice. When internal dissension breaks out among members of the ruling class, an aristocracy (in which the guardians rule under law) degenerates into a timocracy as the military forces, the auxiliaries, clash with the guardian class of rulers and oust the philosopher-kings.

Plato analyzed the character traits developed by the timarch (timocrat) and concluded that the timocratic personality, motivated by an aggressive spirit, is best fitted for war, not for peace. Carried away by his ambition and his passion to excel in all things, the timarch develops a greedy interest in gold, which, once acquired, he lavishes on women and a life of concupiscence. With no regard for genuine culture and with a defiant attitude toward the law, the timarch fears the admission of intellectuals to political office. His only claim to political power is his service as a soldier. This lover of power and honor, this uncultivated character, while obedient to those in authority, abuses the lower classes over whom, in his haughty pride, he lords his superiority. His avaricious nature shows itself in his ever increasing esteem for money. The timocrat's children observe the negative attitude of their father toward cultural pursuits and the law and develop inner conflicts of their own. Caught up in ambition and avaricious appetite, they are pulled in antithetical directions. As a result of these inner conflicts, the sons and daughters of the timocrat fall prey to the influence of unsavory companions—influence which encourages contentiousness, high-spirited passions, arrogance, and aggressiveness. Thus, such people, who lack private property of their own, are increasingly motivated by ambition, compounded by an even lower thirst for wealth. Reason gives way to the passion of ambition. As reason loses ground and as the passion of ambition gains, aristocracy (the rule of what is best) yields to timocracy or timarchy (the rule by venerated victors of battle who have won military fame).

Oligarchy and the Plutocratic Personality. Degeneration from superior to inferior or deteriorating forms of government is due to an erosion of unity in society. Thus, when aristocracy (governed by the philosophical guardians) suffers disunity because of a clash between auxiliary or military class and ruling philosophers, aristocracy degenerates into timocracy. Excessive ambition and greed replace wisdom, the reign of reason. This inversion of values impelled Plato to characterize a timocracy as inferior to an aristocracy.

Timocracy (timarchy), even though it ranks just below an aristocracy, is nevertheless superior to all other forms of government. When it deteriorates, however, the outcome is oligarchy or plutocracy. Oligarchy means rule by a few persons intent on enhancing their own financial gain, while plutocracy means simply rule by the rich. Plato concluded that in practice both amount to the same kind of government, since in both a few wealthy people govern for the sake of their private interests, and the accumulation of wealth is their paramount concern.

Timocracy deteriorates into oligarchy owing to another type of disunity caused by a clash between the rich and poor classes of society. The *Republic* proposed a safeguard against class warfare, namely, a prohibition against the acquisition of property by political leaders. In order to avoid a conflict of interests, the accumulation of wealth was restricted to the merchants, craftsmen, farmers, and other members of the artisan class, the lowest class.

Plato referred to the plutocrats and oligarchs as drones, unproductive and expendable consumers, not producers of goods or providers of services needed by the people. Those who dissipate all their wealth often become stinging drones, criminals or impoverished burdens of society. While the passion of honor transformed aristocracy into timocracy, a passion for wealth reduced timocracy to oligarchy (plutocracy). Whereas the rule of reason (aristocracy) capitulated to the reign of honor (timocracy), the reign of honor succumbed to the desire for wealth. The greed for wealth, however, was bridled by a concern for, or at least a veneer of, respectability.

Plato defined oligarchy in terms of property, as a system in which the rich are powerful, while the poor are prohibited from holding political office. He attributed the collapse of the timocratic state and the decline into oligarchy to the flow of wealth into private hands. Riches and virtue correlate negatively, he said, inasmuch as an increase in the former diminishes the latter. Rivalry and envy rule the day. Laws are manipulated and twisted for the sake of personal financial advantage. Values are inverted; the Platonic virtues are supplanted by vices grounded in excessive desire for wealth. The qualifications and privileges of citizenship are based upon monetary considerations, and the status of the individual is made dependent entirely upon his financial resources. Substantial wealth qualifies a person for political office, and in this way the opportunity to direct the course of the state is left exclusively in their hands.

A plutocracy contains the seeds of its own destruction, inasmuch as each faction, rich and poor, is constantly plotting against the other. Soon any semblance of a unified society ceases as the wealthy dominant class stands in opposition to the poor. Referring to this unavoidable process of disunion, Plato asserted that "such a state is not one, but two states, the one of the poor, and the other of rich men; and they are living on the same spot and always conspiring against one another."[39] Still worse, an oligarchy finds itself incapable of conducting a war, for to wage a war a nation needs more troops than the wealthy class can provide, but if the poor were to be armed they might fight their plutocratic oppressors instead of the foreign enemy. Thus, the dilemma facing the obigarchs is complete: "Either they arm the multitude, and then they are more afraid of them than of the enemy; or, if they do not call them out in the hour of battle, they are oligarchs indeed, few to fight as they are few to rule."[40]

The extremes of great wealth and utter poverty common to oligarchies are both plagues on the nation, for neither the wealthy nor the poor contribute productively to society, either by means of services or goods. Furthermore, "whenever you see paupers in a State," observed Plato, "somewhere in that neighborhood there are hidden away thieves . . . and all sorts of artists in crime."[41] Thus, crime breeds on poverty.

Explaining how people develop from timocratic to oligarchic personality types, Plato traces it from a spirited eagerness to win fame arising from a preponderance of ambition to a lust for money and the gratification of sensual appetite, the catalytic factor being anxiety and feelings of insecurity arising from the humbling effects of poverty. Not only is the head (reason) dethroned, but the heart (will) also capitulates to appetitive desires, desires that may best be gratified through money. Thus both the love of wisdom and the love of ambition (for high honor) are thrust aside in order to acquire property. The personality is in complete upheaval, inasmuch as the lowest aspect of the self (animal appetite) dominates one's mind and ambitions, aspects of a person's higher self. Nevertheless, this type of personality experiences internal conflict arising from his higher desires competing with his lower. True to his oligarchal self, however, this personality type rallies only a small part of himself in this conflict between the higher and lower self, resulting in the lust for wealth conquering the quest for honor or the love of wisdom. Generally, however, his better appetites prevail over the worse. Although a divided personality, the oligarch is in some respects more respectable than many other personality types.

Democracy and the Democratic Type of Personality. Unlike the representative democracies of the modern world, the Athenian democracy, that of a small city-state, accorded equal rights to all adult males over eighteen years of age. Every citizen was privileged to assume any role in government, including the legislative, judicial, and executive bodies. Accordingly, Athenian democracy was a government of amateurs. Sovereignty literally rested with the citizens (excluding minors, females, slaves, and foreigners), except that constitutional laws, binding on everyone, were alterable only by a quorum of six thousand citizens with the concurrence of the *heliaea* (those citizens over thirty years of age who had been certified by the archons as having sworn an oath to uphold the constitution).

Plato regarded democracy as a miscarriage of justice, for his view of justice meant that each person should devote himself solely to the task for which he is best suited by natural aptitude and disposition. Most people, being ill-fitted to govern, should defer that responsibility to those best suited by nature and by training, that is, defer to the few philosophical aristocrats who have realized their highest and noblest nature—wisdom and goodness. Inasmuch as nature is not democratic and does not make everyone equal, so the state should not attempt to introduce an artificial equality. For Plato, a natural aristocracy (not a social aristocracy) should prevail, for all nature operates in this manner. While some persons were both born and trained to rule, others are by nature ill-suited for the task.

Because of inherent defects in oligarchy, it disintegrates into a democracy. As the plutocrats strive to achieve their primary objective to accumulate more wealth, they create conditions which make fewer and fewer people still richer at the expense of the rest of society. The wealthy continue to concentrate wealth in fewer and fewer hands by means of excessive interest rates and other financial devices until at last the masses revolt and overthrow the plutocrats.

Plato asserts that the democratic type of personality, like the oligarchal type, is motivated chiefly by appetitive desires. While the plutocratic personality lusts for money, the democratic personality lusts for the satisfactions of every kind of appetite, for riches and luxuries, for license to do what he pleases free of self-control or restraints. In an oligarchy wealth and power belong to only a few citizens but in a democracy all citizens compete for wealth and power in a free-for-all battle; the most energetic and cunning personalities win the spoils of battle. In the democratic personality sleazy passions ride roughshod over the rational self, appetite rules the head, and emotions displace reason. Impulses and emotion, not enlightened reason, govern both the individual and the state.

The insatiable craving for riches is the catalyst reducing an oligarchy to a democracy. When laws are enacted which encourage prodigality, the youth abandon themselves to extravagance, thereby becoming indebted to the wealthy few. "The rulers," asserted Plato, "being aware that their power rests upon their wealth, refuse to curtail by law the extravagance of the spendthrift youth because they gain by their ruin; they take interest from them and buy up their estates and thus increase their own wealth and importance."[42]

In a society which prizes and honors wealth, the citizens are tempted to relax their self-control. The craving for wealth and the aspiration for self-control are incompatible and create inner conflicts affecting the individual. Because the lust for wealth and the spirit of moderation are mutually conflicting, the impetus of one diminishes the drive of the other, comparable to the action inherent in the law of supply and demand. As supply increases, demand recedes.

The unbridled desire of the oligarchs for riches increases the number of poor people, who become idle beggars, insolvent, disenfranchised, hating the plutocrats to whom they have lost their property, with the result that the masses are ready for a revolution that will bring the wealthy oligarchs down to their own level. Revolution becomes imminent as the plutocrats ignore every possibility of worthwhile community programs of amelioration and become indolent, obese, effeminate, and oblivious to higher motives than their lust for wealth. To preclude the possibility that his ideal state might degenerate into anarchic democracy, Plato, in his *Laws*, banned the practice of usury and the right to demand repayment on loans extended to individuals.

Realizing that the oligarchs in power are feeble and at their mercy, the masses seize the opportunity to revolt. The result is democracy, the state in which each citizen acquires an equal share of freedom and power, of civil rights and the responsibility of serving in the government. In this way the corrupt oligarchy ushers in democracy. The oligarchy, on the verge of collapse, either crumbles or yields to the angry, dissatisfied majority, who utilized violence, armed insurrection, and terror to oust the plutocrats or force them to capitulate.

Cataloging the characteristics of a democracy, Plato commented that "liberty and free speech are rife everywhere; anyone is allowed to do what he likes."[43] A person is free to choose his destiny in a nation openly frank and tolerant. The character traits of its citizens are as varied as the flowers, and so are their manners and opportunities. Its constitution, replete with permissiveness, allows any citizen to rule if he so desires (despite ineptness for the task) or not to be ruled if that be his preference. "There is no compulsion to hold political office," observed Plato, "even if you are qualified, or again, to submit to rule, unless you please, or to go to war when the rest are at war, or to be at peace when others do so, unless you are so disposed; if some law forbids you to hold office or be a judge, you may nevertheless do both if it strikes your fancy. Is not all this a heavenly and supremely delightful life, while it lasts?"[44] Tolerance abounds everywhere. Even convicted criminals placidily stroll about the city despite their having been sentenced to death or exile. Continuing in this vein of ironic humor, Plato mentioned the forgiving spirit inherent in a democracy. He noted democracy's "disdain for all those fine principles we laid down in founding our commonwealth (the philosophical aristocracy), as when we said that, except in the case of some rarely gifted nature, one would never become a good man unless from childhood his play and all his pursuits were concerned with things fair and good. How grandly does democracy trample all these fine notions of ours underfoot, never giving a thought to the pursuits which make a statesman. It honors anyone who merely calls himself the people's friend."[45] Viewing democracy as a pleasant form of anarchy (a government without leaders), Plato considered it a "charming form of government, full of variety and disorder, and dispensing a sort of equality to equals and unequals alike."[46] In a democracy, he said, unfit people govern while all standards of good taste and principles essential for an orderly state are entirely disregarded.

Despotism and the Tyrannical Personality. Just as the democratic personality emerges from the oligarchic type, the tyrannical personality grows out of the degenerate democratic type. Now the result, said Plato, is despotism, the ultimate stage in the deterioration of the commonwealth. The tyrant, a dictator with absolute power, is not bound by any law or constitution. He may be a benevolent dictator or a vicious despot, but in either case people have lost their liberty and are relegated to slavery.

In an anarchic democracy, the individual as well as the majority indulge their wild desires promiscuously, without discretion, regard for order, or concern for a priority of values. Bombarded with conflicting desires, and lacking any unanimity of values or consensus, the nation is split into three major conflicting factions which tear the state apart; the ruined oligarchs or spendthrifts now living as desperadoes; the plutocrats or wealthy capitalists; and the peasant masses spread over the countryside tending their farms but without any interest in politics. Unless they were bribed by an offer of material gain for themselves, the peasants, who could gain supreme power if united, will never get together for mobilization and control of the state.

License, the insatiable craving for complete freedom of action, is the catalyst that reduces democracy to tyranny. The passion for freedom converts whatever semblance of order might exist in a democracy into the disorder of anarchy. Once the minds of the citizens have mistaken license for liberty, the same error afflicts the entire state and corrupts its other values: "There is a conflict and they gain the day; reverence and awe they call foolishness . . . ; temperance they nickname effeminateness, and abuse it and repudiate it; they teach that moderation and orderly expenditure are vulgar and miserly; and so, by the help of a rabble of vile appetites, they expel them over the border."[47] These virtues vanish, to be replaced by such vices as insolence, anarchy, prodigality, and impudence. Plato continued: "Insolence they euphemistically call good breeding, and anarchy liberty, and waste munificence, and impudence courage."[48] The upshot of the matter is that a youth who should have been trained in the school of necessity, responding only to those necessary pleasures that sustain and maintain the body, becomes a libertine, yielding to whatever lustful temptation happens his way.

Thus, said Plato, an unprincipled people create an unprincipled state with an unprincipled ruler—a despot. It is the insatiable lust for freedom to the complete neglect of all other values that cultivates the soil of libertinism from which tyrants sprout. The elimination of law and order is mistaken for joy and freedom. In their disregard for principles and standards the democratic citizens themselves take on the characteristics of a tyrant. The outcome is that man and state are alike—a tyrannical personality and despotic state. In this manner democracy deteriorates into tyranny.

Describing the manner in which democracy degenerates into tyranny, Plato says that out of a spirit of freedom and equality young people consider themselves to be the equal of their parents, whom they therefore no longer look up to or respect. Law-abiding citizens are mocked and insulted and laughed at as nonentities. Anarchy pervades the classroom while students show disrespect for their instructors and become argumentative as if they possessed sufficient knowledge to justify disputing their teachers. Instead of condemning such impudence and arrogance, adult citizens surrender their authoritative views and imitate the young, fearful that otherwise they will be regarded as obnoxious tyrants.

The process of imposing tyranny upon the people begins when a single champion arises in their midst who purports to be the protector of their interests. He poses as one who will take money and property from the rich and distribute them to the poor, but actually contrives to seize the lion's share for himself. Impeachments, judgments, and all sorts of litigation become commonplace as the masses appeal to their champion for action serving their greedy purposes. He agrees to be the people's advocate, then emerges as their protector.

His transformation from protector to tyrant, however, occurs when, having successfully despoiled one victim, he shows his true voracious character and, with mobs at his disposal, casts all scruples to the wind, attacking everyone in his way with false accusations that result in execution or exile or in some cases in murder. At the same time, in order to sustain popular support for himself, he implies that he is about to partition the lands of the wealthy and abolish all debts.

His next move is the mobilization of a private army. He begins by requesting bodyguards on the pretext that his enemies are conspiring to assassinate him, and then, when he obtains the guards, he adds more and more of them to sustain and increase his power. The state may send him off to foreign lands for a time, but eventually he will return, boast of his exploits abroad to restore his waning popularity at home, and exercise power in a despotic manner to crush his enemies and maintain unchallenged authority over the nation. He keeps the nation at war to perpetuate his ironclad rule. He augments his military forces to control dissidents, purging even those who had loyally helped him to establish the dictatorship. "The tyrant," asserted Plato, "must get rid of them; he cannot stop while he has a friend or an enemy who is good for anything."[49] Since any worthy person must be eliminated, his purges reduce the country to an intellectually, physically, and morally bankrupt condition.

Soon only the lowest elements of society remain; and they must give the tyrant absolute devotion and loyalty; the outcome is a nation of slaves. He will then rape the nation of its treasures, confiscating whatever wealth he can lay his hands on, riches which for a time enable him to reduce the tax burdens of the people; but when the plunder is exhausted, he turns upon his closest associates, even his own father, and fatherland. The despot, lamented Plato, "is a parricide, and a cruel guardian of an aged parent; and this is real tyranny . . . : the people, in attempting to escape the smoke of servitude to free men, have fallen into the fire of enslavement to slaves. Thus liberty, getting out of all order and reason, passes into the harshest and bitterest form of slavery."[50]

The degeneration which occurs in society is paralleled by the same corruption occurring within the personality of the individual as he subordinates wisdom to his passions. The personality, instead of being ruled by the rational self, the self controlling desires by allowing only their wholesome expression, is now governed by irrational lust, the lowest possible trait of character. Plato regarded this perversion of the personality as a form of insanity, because the irrational aspects of the personality dictate to and control its rational aspects and its entire structure.

VII *Precursor of the Hegelian Dialectic: The Platonic Dialectic*

Every action has its reaction, but the more severe or extreme the action, then the more definite the reaction. Stating the matter in Hegelian terms, each thesis has its antithesis, and the more extreme the thesis, the more violently will the pendulum swing to its antithesis. Although this dialectical logic was attributed to Hegel, it appears to have originated with Plato, who saw that when a form of government is excessively extreme, it rebounds to its opposite, that is, to an antithetical form of government. Plato perceptively remarked: "The ruin of oligarchy is the ruin of democracy; the same disease magnified and intensified by liberty [permissiveness or license] enslaves democracy—the truth being that the excessive increase in anything usually causes a reaction in the opposite direction. This is the case not only in weather, in plants, in bodies, but most especially in political societies."[51] Thus, the Hegelian dialectic has its roots in the Platonic dialectic. The indebtedness of Marx to Plato's political philosophy is also evident.

CHAPTER 6

Philosophy of Education

PLATO'S philosophy of education stems from his political philosophy, since in the latter education is regarded as providing the training needed to become a good citizen. Training for citizenship entails considerably more than educating statesmen to assume positions of leadership, for basic to any kind of training (including craftsmanship) is schooling in the moral life. Ethics and its complement, social ethics, is the critical factor in the good life, both personal and social. Without morality, especially justice, a nation cannot survive. Even more, an individual's mental health is contingent on it and the other virtues or excellences.

The aim of education, then, is the production of social-minded citizens who are happy because they have found their life occupations suited to their natures, their aptitudes, and their dispositions. The aim of education is to ascertain for which career a person should be trained; it is therefore designed to make people moral and good and wholesome, physically, morally, mentally, vocationally, and socially. Plato regarded education as the one great principle.

Good political and individual constitutions, both physical and mental, are due to a good education. By it the perfect state comes into existence together with the individual, who is the mirror image of the nation. Education is essentially a process whereby justice and injustice develop in societies.

Education and nurture were of paramount importance to Plato, who held that society, "if it once starts well, proceeds as it were in a cycle of growth. Good education and upbringing if kept up will lead to people of a better nature, and these in turn, taking advantage of such education, will improve with each generation."[1] Accordingly, those responsible for the education of society must be vigilant lest corruption in the process of education arise without their becoming aware of it.

114

Successful education and its prime objective, whether physical education or a knowledge of the fine or liberal arts, serve the same end, namely, moral growth and improvement of the personality in order that the society and its constituents may emerge just and happy. Music, gymnastics, logic or dialectic, and other academic disciplines serve a moral goal, the good of individuals and the society that they comprise. Thus moral training of both citizens and rulers is the primary concern of education in both the *Republic* and the *Laws*. In stressing the development of good citizens, Plato had in mind people both obedient and loyal to the nation's constitution.

I *The Curriculum*

In an earlier chapter mention was made that formal education was intended only for Athenian boys and that girls were virtually excluded. Whatever education girls acquired was received from women in the home. Boys, though living at home, had a more formal sort of education through daily attendance in private schools. The state did not provide instruction, for that responsibility fell to the boy's family. Plato rejected the customary practice of special education for boys; he insisted that girls should receive the same education as boys. Not only should girls enjoy equal education but they should have equal job opportunities as well.

Plato disagreed with Solon and others who held that an aged person can still learn many things efficiently. Training in learning, argued Plato, is comparable to training in gymnastics; it belongs to the young. An older citizen, he claimed, is even less able to learn than to run a race.

A second Platonic caveat had to do with the use of coercion in education. The mind, being free, cannot be subject to compulsion as if it were a slave. Knowledge gained under duress is easily lost. The only education that is worthwhile is that which is enjoyed as an exciting game. Only in this way can one discern whether or not a person has a natural bent for learning.

II *Graded Education: Platonic Stages*

In brief, the successive grades or stages of education as Plato prescribed them are as follows: (1) From entry into school at ten until the age of seventeen or eighteen, children will be tutored in music, literature, physical education, and elementary mathematics. (2) From seventeen until twenty, youths undergo intensive training in compulsory physical and military education, leaving virtually no time for academic studies. (3) From twenty to thirty years of age, a decade of advanced mathematical sciences is pursued. Plato considered these disciplines highly advisable as preparation for the study of dialectics. For dialectical understanding students must be taught how to coordinate their knowledge of studies that were heretofore taught segmentally. The various academic disciples must be comprehended as a unified whole. Training of this character will enable students to view the body of knowledge synoptically, interrelatedly, and as a whole, rather than merely absorbing bits of uncorrelated data. It is the person with synoptic insight who is dialectically astute. The best criterion of a dialectical nature is for a person to be able to view things as a coherent and systematic whole. While "synoptic" means the ability to view the pertinent connections that hold, "dialectic" signifies the ability to reason logically.

(4) From thirty to thirty-five years of age, the selection process continues, and those chosen devote themselves entirely to dialectic, particularly with respect to the philosophical apprehension of the Good and other ultimate moral principles. The test for this group is the ability to view things abstractly (devoid of sense data). (5) From thirty-five to fifty, on-the-job training is undertaken by the guardians who will acquire practical experience in subordinate posts of public service. (6) Beginning at age fifty, the intellectual aristocracy, having attained the vision of the absolute Good, serve as a supreme governing council. Although the pursuit of philosophy is to remain their chief pursuit, they are expected to serve their term of office in politics as well, ruling in the interest of public good.

III *The Educational Curriculum of the Guardian Class*

To a considerable extent, Plato followed the curriculum format that was in vogue in his time. But he did make modifications, especially by eliminating those elements that failed to generate his guardian type of personality, a morally and mentally healthy individual as well as an educated one.

The primary curriculum consisted of (1) gymnastic, exercises in athletics; (2) music, education in the liberal as well as the fine arts, including philosophy, culture, music, art, letters; (3) grammatic, learning to read and to write; and (4) mathematic, elementary forms of it. Early education was supposed to be an enjoyable experience, a sort of amusement rather than the drudgery of compulsion. While compulsion is acceptable in physical gymnastics, where it does no harm, it fails with respect to academic studies, for knowledge acquired through force is not retained.

Early education, beginning at about the age of ten, was conducted in the country away from adverse parental influence, for Plato sought an environment conducive to his educational philosophy. Plato divided the curriculum for the earliest years into gymnastic and music (including literature), the former for the development of the body, and the latter for the development of the personality. Music (and literature), however, precedes gymnastics.

Literature. For purposes of education, the early years are critical in the formation of personality, for it is then that a human being is most impressionable. For this reason, fiction, which is replete with deleterious falsehoods, is to be placed under censorship. Mythological tales, because they are immoral, are likewise censored. Theological instruction must maintain the goodness and justice of God, teaching that he, as the author of good, is good as well as true. Evil must be ascribed to an alien source, a factor other than God. Because they are ridden with lies, the works of the great poets, such as Homer and Aeschylus, must be repudiated.

Theological literature which incites fear must be rejected, because the virtue of courage cannot be cultivated in a person who is overwhelmed with the fear of death and of the hell to follow. Good persons need not fear death, or anything else (except immorality) either in this life or the next.

Although a high priority is placed upon truth, if anyone is to have the privilege of lying, it must be allowed the rulers, and only when it is for the public good. Plato compares this with the physician who administers medicine deceitfully to his patient in order to restore him to health. This teaching seems to be the only Machiavellian notion in Platonic philosophy.

Another peculiarity in Plato's philosophy of education is the injunction against uncontrollable laughter, for he believes that violent laughter has a tendency to provoke violent reactions: "A fit of laughter which has been indulged to excess almost always produces a violent reaction."[2] Plato observed that when an individual succumbs to uncontrollable laughter, a vehement alteration of mood usually follows. In order to curb this emotion from lapsing into excess, distinguished and honored people must be used as models or examples of those who can control their emotion.

Comparable training must be given with respect to self-control, for guardians must be able to restrain their concupiscent desire for voluptuous pleasures of sex, food, and drink. The literature to which people are exposed glorifies immoderate behavior and self-indulgence, and must therefore be censored. On the other hand, deeds of endurance and other examples of self-control by famous personalities should be both witnessed and read.

The upshot of the matter is that literature and stories that do no more than cultivate a tolerance for evil in the young must come to an end. "Therefore," declared Plato, "let us put an end to such tales, lest they engender laxity of morals among the young."[3]

Plato imposed strictures prohibiting guardian trainees from resorting to dramatic recitation, for he wanted them to be creators rather than followers, to devote their undivided attention to the task of their particular craft of maintaining the freedom of the state, and not to acquire the personality traits of the unsavory characters that they mimic or continually reenact. If these fledgling guardians must engage in dramatic recitation, soliloquizing, impersonating, or other forms of imitation, they should dramatically represent (mimesis) personages of the finest character and breeding instead of the ravings of madmen, abnormal women, slaves, the unfortunate, or anyone else whose character would demean one's own station, personality, or career. An actor at best is a secondhand character, trying to be other than he is, hence a lie, for he is not true to himself. Guardians must not only be genuine, but they must lead creative lives instead of remaining in the shadow of someone else.

In his discussion of mimesis ("imitation" or "identification"), Plato anticipated the Freudian mechanism of identification. He knew the pleasure derived by a spectator from identifying with the character or hero that he admires. What troubled Plato was that through imaginative identification a person may come to be like the character imitated, but the fancied hero imitated is often an insidious villain who is not recognized as such by unsuspecting youth. Plato's theory of imitation also anticipated the work of the psychologist Albert Bandura, who has done considerable work on imitation and modeling theory. Plato noted that most models selected from folklore have a deleterious effect on one—comparable to the effects of certain television shows on the youth of today. Plato was also disturbed about *mimesis* and modeling, because he felt that if a person devotes a considerable portion of his time (if not a complete lifetime) to playacting, he will never develop into an authentic individual with a life and calling that are distinctively and genuinely his own.

Music. Considering music a most potent vehicle of education, Plato called for a harmony of soul and body. To him it was the fairest of sights. "When a man's soul has a beautiful character, and his body matches it in beauty and is thus in harmony with it," asserted Plato, "that harmonizing combination, bearing the same stamp of beauty, is the most beautiful sight for anyone who has eyes to see it."[4]

While Plato approved of the age-old Athenian practice of writing lyric poetry for the purpose of singing it to musical accompaniment, and vice versa, he insisted that rhythm and melody must follow the words. Plato disapproved of the distortion of lyrics by wrenching them to match the music, a practice that was viewed with increasing disfavor by Athenians.

Harmony was of critical importance to Plato, who regarded it, as he also regarded justice, as the necessary balance for individual mental health as well as for the health of society. Harmony in the individual soul has a concomitant harmonizing effect on society; it possesses a socializing influence. The ultimate objective of education is the attainment of insight into the harmonious world order, inasmuch as the world is a harmoniously ordered cosmos rather than a discordant chaos: "Musical training is a more potent instrument than any other, because rhythm and harmony permeate the inner recesses of the soul and take the strongest hold upon it, making a person gracious if he has been rightly trained, or of him who is ill-educated crude."[5] Education in the beauties of music equip an individual so that he readily perceives ugliness wherever it may be found and responds to it with disgust, but at the same time he recognizes and approves loveliness, which cultivates a noble spirit within his personality.

The outcome of education in music and poetry is the appreciation and love of beauty. By learning to sense and appreciate beauty the individual makes a transition from the primary stages of education to the higher, intellectual, or more sophisticated forms. The love of beauty, like all true love, is free from sensuality. "True love is a love of beauty and order—temperate and harmonious."[6] Intemperance is a form of madness that should not be confused with true love.

Physical Education: Gymnastics. An education in music is followed by gymnastics or physical training. As is the case with music, gymnastics should begin in the early years, but it must continue throughout life. Although Plato believed in a sound mind in a sound body, he contested the theory that "a sound and healthy body is enough to produce a sound mind." On the other hand, however, "a sound mind has internal power to render the physical condition as improved as possible."[7] It is advisable, therefore, to entrust the care of the body to well-trained minds that have proved capable of caring for themselves. Hence Plato has anticipated psychosomatic medicine.

Plato, who disapproved of the physical exercises of athletes of his time, recommended a simple form of military gymnastics for the warrior class. Athletes, complained Plato, engage in such gross training practices that they "sleep away their lives," and are easy prey to illness. By contrast, the military must be alert and vigilant, capable of maintaining health despite extreme changes in weather conditions. Simplicity, rather than excess and erratic changes in eating, sleeping, and other habits, is the rule of their lives. A simple diet and moderate exercise will suffice.

People of a sound mind, who care for themselves intelligently (physically, mentally, and morally) could and should be their own physicians and lawyers. Instead of constantly engaging in litigation, these people can settle their differences without appealing for a court decision. Plato spoke disparagingly of "the evil in which a man is not only a lifelong litigant, passing all his days in the courts, either as plaintiff or defendant, but is actually led by his bad taste to pride himself on his litigiousness; he fancies that he is an expert in dishonesty; able to take every crooked turn, and wriggle into and out of every loophole."[8] Plato thought it considerably more desirable to order one's life so as to avoid the necessity of appearing before a "drowsy judge." He attributed this turn of events to the disgracefully low state of education. While the lower classes of laborers resort to judges and physicians, those with a proper liberal education should have a better alternative. Plato thought it contemptible that educated people should be so lacking in any sense of justice that they turn to judges for it, thus making judges their critics and masters. In this respect, Plato was anticipating the views of St. Paul.

Athletes exercise to increase muscular strength, but Plato valued exercise as a means of stimulating the spirit. Thus the case for music holds also for gymnastic activities; both serve the purpose of improving the person, his inner self. It is not true, therefore, that music trains the mind while exercise trains the body.

Plato warned, however, that care should be exercised so that musical education will not be stressed too much for it will then produce a soft and effeminate personality; nor should physical exercise be overemphasized, for it will lead to hardness, brutality, or ferocity. One discipline, however, balances the other: the coarse athlete can be refined by music, and the philosophic disposition can be tempered by exercise. These two branches of learning should blend into the curriculum in order to achieve a well-balanced personality.

The fine arts and gymnastic activities work toward the same end, the improvement of the personality, psychologically and morally, by harmonizing or balancing the intellectual or philosophical self with the spirited self: "To put these two sorts of minds, the spirited and the philosophic, into agreement, heaven has given mankind these two branches of education, music and gymnastic, not for the sake of soul and body (except incidentally), but for the harmonious adjustment of these two with each other. . . . The one who best blends gymnastic with music and applies them most suitably to the personality may be rightly called complete in music and a harmonious person."[9] Consequently, musical education as well as physical education serve to make a person better psychologically and morally, rather than merely being a source of amusement.

Higher Education: Mathematics. Mathematics marks a transitional point in the guardian's education, for it is via mathematical principles that the human mind makes its passage from the material world of sense to the ultimately real world of thought, that is, from appearance to reality. The psyche turns from the accumulation of material gain to the pursuit of wisdom, from a dependence on the senses to a reliance on the intellect. Rather than a concern for tangible objects, higher mathematics deals with abstractions, not things but thoughts.

While simple arithmetic will do for merchants, retail-traders, and the masses, it will not suffice for the guardians, both those who legislate and those who guard the nation. As philosophers, the legislators and rulers require abstract mathematical training as a means of rising out of the sea of material things to the realm of values—to the domain of reality and of the Good. It is vital that they ascertain the Good for the enhancement of the state. Although the Good is attained through dialectical intuition, the highest stage of cognition leading up to it is mathematical reasoning, that is, coping with abstract objects. The reason for the indispensability of mathematics toward this end is that it requires the mind to arrive at conclusions (pure truth) by the sheer exercise of pure thought. For these reasons, mathematics should be the first study of the guardians.

Up to this point, education did not demand intellection, but merely the use of the senses. Sense perception does not provoke thought, but mental judgment regarding what is sensed does. It is when our senses provide us with confusing and contradictory data that we are driven to mental reflection concerning such sensa.

In prescribing mathematical studies, Plato listed them in the following order: (1) arithmetic; (2) geometry; (3) solid geometry; (4) astronomy; and (5) harmonics. If a sixth subject of higher education, dialectic, were to be added, the program of studies would be complete.

Dialectic. Higher education in the mathematical sciences as listed above was offered to guardians from twenty to thirty years of age. After a decade of mathematical instruction, dialectic followed for those thirty to thirty-five years of age who proved themselves capable of abstract reasoning. Whereas mathematics deals with deductive reasoning from assumed premises, dialectic is a means of viewing entities synoptically by immediate intuition of reality. A dialectician is a person who can explain or offer an account of reality. While others live in a world of dreams about reality, the dialectician possesses a waking view of it. Instead of illustrating truth allegorically, the dialectician ascertains the truth as it really is. By dialectic the thing as it truly is in itself is known.

Dialectic is the highest mode of cognition; the three inferior modes in descending order are thinking, believing, and imagining. (Dialectic will be discussed further in our final chapter.)

IV   *Learning as Recollection*

Plato based his theory of learning as recollection *(anamnēsis)* on a view of the immortality of the mind; he then argued that what we learn is simply a recollection of what we acquired from an earlier life when we dwelt in the Ideal world of reality. Inasmuch as everything in the world is interrelated, once a person recollects any particular part, he can (through the process of association) recall the rest, provided that he exerts sufficient effort.

Although the theory of the association of ideas is a modern concept often attributed to John Locke, the concept actually originated with Plato, who viewed it as "associative recollection." In Plato's *Phaedo*, we read: "What is the feeling of lovers when they recognize a lyre, or a garment, or anything else which the beloved has been in the habit of using? Do they not, from knowing the lyre, form in the mind's eye an image of the youth to whom the lyre belongs? This is recollection. In like manner any one who sees Simmias may remember Cebes; and there are endless examples of the same thing."[10]

As previously stated, Plato's recollection theory of learning is premised on the soul's immortality, but Plato saw the doctrine of recollection as implying an earlier existence. Inasmuch as the soul existed prior to its coming to earth, it should be able to survive after its sojourn upon earth is concluded.

The inability to learn, then, must be attributed to a faulty memory or to factors which becloud the memory. While memory is the preservation of sensation, recollection is the recovery of it. In distinguishing the two, Plato wrote: "When that which has been experienced by the soul in common with the body is recaptured, so far as may be, by and in the soul itself apart from the body, then we speak of recollecting something. . . . And further, when the soul that has lost the memory of a sensation or what it has learned resumes that memory within itself and goes over the old ground, we regularly speak of these processes as recollections."[11]

The question that Plato is raising here is that if the human mind can think of real objects that it never experienced in this life on earth, how did man originally acquire such knowledge? All *a priori* knowledge falls into this category. The Pythagorean theorem, for example, or any of the other geometrical notions that the mind entertains without the aid of the senses, is of this character. Plato is asking how it is possible for anyone to discover new truths while sitting alone with eyes shut and without any other contact with the external world? Such knowledge, obviously hidden deep in the recesses of the mind, is brought to consciousness. The process of raising this unconscious knowledge to the conscious level of the mind, Plato termed "recollection." Plato also regarded as innate the mind's ability to reason deductively or mathematically; even value concepts are innate.

To prove his theory of learning by recollection, Plato describes Socrates' method of eliciting geometrical knowledge from an entirely uneducated boy, the slave of Meno, who is involved in a discussion on recollection theory with Socrates. Merely by questioning the lad, Socrates believes that he has elicited from him (without supplying any information) truths in the field of geometry. The Socratic contention is that the geometrical knowledge displayed by the boy was possible only because of his knowledge of them prior to birth. Accordingly, the truths were not produced, much less instilled; they were recalled.

While certain modes of learning can be classified as recollection, the question arises as to whether all knowledge is reducible to a mere matter of reminiscence. It appears that Plato so concluded, judging from the following dialogue between Meno and Socrates:

Yes, Socrates; but what do you mean by saying that we do not learn, and that what we call learning is only a process of recollection? Can you teach me this?

I told you Meno, just now that you were a rogue, and now you ask whether I can teach you, when I am saying that there is no teaching, but only recollection.[12]

It is at this point that Meno's slave boy is introduced, from whom Socrates extracts certain mathematical conclusions that the lad has never been taught before. Through Socratic dialogue, that is, the technique of asking questions without furnishing the answers, the boy arrives at certain correct conclusions, including the principle that a square of a diagonal is double the square of the side.

The following charming conversation between the slave boy and Socrates deals with the method of proving that the square of a diagonal is double the square of one side. (Keep in mind that considerable conversation has taken place up to this point establishing a basis for the dialogue.)

SOCRATES. Mark now, starting from this state of development, I shall only ask him, and not teach him, and he shall share the enquiry with me: and do you watch and see if you find me telling or explaining anything to him, instead of eliciting his opinion. Tell me, boy, is not this a square of four feet which I have drawn? [1, 2, 3, 4]

BOY. Yes.
SOCRATES. Now we can add another square equal to it like this? [2, 3, 5, 6]

BOY. Yes.
SOCRATES. And a third, which is equal to them? [3, 5, 7, 8]

BOY. Yes.
SOCRATES. Suppose we fill up the vacant corner? [4, 3, 8, 9]

BOY. Very good.
SOCRATES. Here, then, are four equal squares?
BOY. Yes.
SOCRATES. And how many times larger is this space than the first square?
BOY. Four times.
SOCRATES. But we want one double the size, as you will remember.
BOY. True.
SOCRATES. Does not this line, reaching from corner to corner, cut each of the squares in half?

BOY. Yes.

SOCRATES. And are there not four equal lines enclosing this area? [2, 5, 8, 4]

BOY. There are.

SOCRATES. Look and see. How large is this area?

BOY. I do not understand.

SOCRATES. Has not the interior line cut off half of the four spaces?

BOY. Yes.

SOCRATES. And how many halves are there in this section? [2, 5, 8, 4]

BOY. Four

SOCRATES. And how many in this? [1, 2, 3, 4]

BOY. Two.

SOCRATES. And four is how many times two?

BOY. Two.

SOCRATES. And the figure is how many feet?

BOY. Eight feet.

SOCRATES. And from what line do you get this figure?

BOY. From this one.

SOCRATES. That is, from the line which extends from corner to corner of the square of four feet?

BOY. Yes.

SOCRATES. And that is the line that is technically called diagonal; and if we employ that name, then you, Meno's slave, are prepared to affirm that the square of the diagonal of the original square is double its area?

BOY. Certainly, Socrates.

SOCRATES. What do you think, Meno? Were not all these answers given out of his own head?

MENO. Yes, they were all his own.

SOCRATES. And yet, as we were saying a few minutes ago, he did not know?

MENO. True.

SOCRATES. But still he had in him those notions of his. Had he not?
MENO. Yes.
SOCRATES. But these notions were somewhere in him, were they not?
MENO. Yes.
SOCRATES. Consequently, he who does not know has in himself true notions on a subject without having knowledge?
MENO. He has.
SOCRATES. At present these notions have just been stirred up in him, as in a dream; but if he were frequently asked the same questions, in different ways, you can see that eventually he will have as accurate a knowledge on the matter as anyone else?
MENO. I dare say.
SOCRATES. Without anyone teaching him he will recover his knowledge for himself, if he is only asked questions?
MENO. Yes.
SOCRATES. And this spontaneous recovery of knowledge in him is *recollection*.[13]

In the foregoing dialogue, Socrates does not assume that he has taught Meno that learning is nothing more than recollection, for the simple reason that Meno will have to recollect that truth for himself. Otherwise learning would not be recollection. The Socratic lesson, if it teaches nothing else, establishes the fact that if a student is to learn, he must actively learn for himself. To pour facts into students is a vain pedagogical effort. What must be done is to elicit thoughts from them; otherwise they will lack the necessary understanding that makes knowledge meaningful. The Socratic dialectic of eliciting information by posing carefully phrased questions is a most effective method of instruction, but it is virtually a lost art in contemporary education. Rather than being passively instructed, one should actively learn. A teacher is simply a *facilitator*.

Plato formulated his doctrine of *anamnesis*, the theory of learning as recollection, to explain how one apprehends *a priori* truths. Conversation did not give the slave boy information, but merely helped him to recollect his geometry, and in the same way it helped Meno to recollect what learning is; Socrates was not actually teaching either of them. The learning that occurred in Meno and his slave is the same type of learning *(anamnesis)* that occurs in any human being, that is, the ability to learn by recollection—which for both Socrates and Plato meant *reminiscence* of knowledge acquired in a previous existence in the heavenly world of *Ideas*.

CHAPTER 7

Philosophy of Religion

P LATO'S metaphysics is deeply concerned with concepts that
play a major role in the philosophy of religion. His influence on
philosophical thinkers must not be regarded as limited to neo-
platonists and traditional Christian scholars, such as St. Augustine,
for his ideas have penetrated into the twentieth century, as is evidenced by the major influence his ideas have had upon distinguished philosophers, for example, Alfred North Whitehead. Especially is this noticeable in Whitehead's process philosophy. Plato's
influence on Whitehead can also be seen in Whitehead's theories
about the primordial nature of God (the eternal and immutable
Ideals of Plato) and the consequent nature of God (the receptacle
and Becoming elements of Platonic theory).

I Synopsis of Plato's Natural Theology

The orderly world (*kosmos*), that is, the physical universe, Plato
regarded as generated (*genesis*) rather than as eternal like the Ideas.
It is generated because it is perceptible by the senses, hence corporeal. While God created (or more accurately fashioned) the generated world (the world of Becoming or phenomena), he did not
create the immutable Ideas that are coeternal with him. Actually,
God, the *Demiurge* (literally one who works for the people), did not
even create matter per se, for he found brute matter unformed in
the Receptacle (*dexamenē*) or empty space (*chora*). The Deity is
essentially a world-forming God. The Receptacle or Space is coeternal with God as are the Ideals. Consequently, God is a world-
builder, a world-designer, or an artistic, skilled worker rather than a
Creator-God in the Judeo-Christian sense of the word.

The "matter" with which God worked, owing to its nature, placed
many restrictions on what God could do with it, for it had its limita-

128

tions, as we shall see shortly. "Matter" is not a technically correct term to use with respect to Platonic philosophy, for the word came into currency with Aristotle's use of it for the stuff or substance forming the physical world. The Platonic term for matter (or as close as it is possible to approach it) is "Receptacle" or "space."

Because it is neither a perception nor a conception, space is unknowable either by sense or by thought. Hence it is neither a phenomenal manifestation nor a Platonic Idea. It simply is devoid of Being, and is termed by Plato Not-Being. It is the Receptacle of phenomena transpiring in the temporal world. Without space, Being (reality) could not become apparent to the senses; the universal Ideas could not become individual objects; mental realities could not participate in the world of existence. Perhaps one might think of space as the blackboard that receives the written word; the board per se is not the word, yet without it words could not be produced. The physical world is contained within space and time, as if these were the requisite elements constituting the physical world. In other words, the world of phenomena (Becoming) is the world that is sensed or perceived as being in some place and at some time. Actually, what God did was to bring order out of disorder, a cosmos out of chaos, by designing things according to a Pattern or paradigm (*paradeigma*) that he contemplates.

Since matter has its limitations (one being the impossibility of making anything absolutely perfect out of it), the physical world must be imperfect. Hence God is the author of an imperfect universe. Why should God trouble himself to create an imperfect world? Does not God do only that which is perfect? Plato's answer is a simple one. God's criterion of creation is not perfection but goodness. If God should inquire of himself, Should I create a world? the determining factor would not be: Only if it is perfect. Rather, the decisive criterion would be: Provided it is good. For God goodness is not only the criterion of creation, but also the goal of all creation. Goodness is the motivating factor of the world and its inhabitants.

Motion, motivation, or movement is a necessity if the world is to move toward its goals. Inert matter would leave us with a dead world devoid of activity. Consequently, God infused a soul into the world (world-soul) as well as into individual bodies that are regarded as living things. There is in the human being, however, a cognitive soul that is imperishable, a soul that is eternal. It is precisely this eternal soul that enables human beings to acertain knowledge which transcends the ability of sense perception. Such transcendental knowledge of the Ideal world of reality is contained deep in the unconscious resources of this rational soul. Evidently, this soul must have undergone a preexistence to acquire such knowledge. By virtue of this soul's being independent of the physical realm, it will enjoy a postexistence as well, returning in immortality to the real world of Ideals, where it will become an inhabitant of a perfect world.

II   The Pattern (Ideal Being), Receptacle (Space), and Generation (Creation)

In establishing the foundations of his philosophy of religion, Plato predicated his natural theology on three categories: (1) the Pattern, (2) the Receptacle, and (3) the Generated. These three entities were required in order for God to bring into existence the world as we know it. Of them Plato wrote:

This new beginning of our discussion of the universe requires a fuller division than the former; for then we made two classes, now a third must be revealed. The two sufficed for the former discussion: one, which we assumed, was a *Pattern* intelligible and always the same; and the second was only the imitation of the pattern, *Generated* and visible. There is also a third kind. . . . What nature are we to attribute to this new kind of being? We reply, that it is the *Receptacle*, and in a manner the nurse, of all generation.[1]

Thus Plato viewed the universe as trichotomized into three principal realms: (1) the realm of the Pattern by which God designed the world; (2) the category of the Receptacle, the space dimension of the world that received created things; and (3) the Generated or created objects, replicas of the Pattern of Ideals, that were in continuous development in the Receptacle.

The Pattern (Paradeigma). The Platonic Ideas or Forms are eternal transcendent archetypes or Patterns *(paradeigma).* The Greek term *paradeigma* means a pattern, a model, a plan, an example, or a paradigm. For Plato, it meant the heavenly plan or ideal by which to pattern all things on earth either by God or man. "No State can be happy," wrote Plato in the *Republic,* "which is not designed by artists who imitate the heavenly Pattern."[2]

Plato spoke of Forms or Ideas (Ideals) as Patterns. Objects in the physical universe imitate these Patterns, for they are copies of them. Forms or Ideas are more than essences (ultimately real entities); they are archetypes providing the design for the phenomenal world. Otherwise the phenomenal world would lack order, direction, and purpose. Although Platonic Forms transcend phenomenal objects, with a reality far beyond them, they also are immanent in phenomenal objects. Moreover, created objects of the phenomenal world participate in the Forms; the greater the participation, the more beautiful or perfected they become. The presence *(parousia)* of Ideas in created things is important, for the greater the presence of Forms in phenomena, the better they are. The greater the presence of the Ideal of justice in a state, the more just the state.

The Receptacle. The Receptacle, also called by Plato "space without bounds," is the primodial chaos out of which God organizes a cosmos, an orderly, purposeful world. The Receptacle not only accommodates or receives the generated elements of creation (phenomena) but also serves as the locus of creation. As such the Receptacle is indeterminate, acquiring its formation from the Ideals or prototypes *(paradeigma)*. Out of disorder raging in the Receptacle, God effects order; out of inertia, God infuses the world with life and movement, with motion serving as the causal factor. God has transformed chaotic motion into order. It is due to the Receptacle that eternal souls acquire embodiment. Were it not for such embodiment, souls could not be particularized, that is, one person could not be recognized from another.

While the Good is the purpose of creation, the energy for creation is God. The Receptacle, however, is also vital, for it is the locus of creation. Without it there would be no place for God to effect his creation. It should be kept in mind that creation is that which is generated, in a constant process of development, and eventually perishes before attaining perfection. It is the Receptacle, unlimited space, that is fit to receive events and the myriad of objects that strive to copy or imitate the primordial Ideals.

While the Receptacle is a void (Not-Being), it is a determinate void; that is, it is the spatial and temporal setting in which all phenomena occur. Unlike boundless space, time is not eternal, but created. The events that occur in space, however, are defined by the Pattern rather than by the Receptacle, the Receptacle providing but a seat *(ēdra)* for generation or creation.

The multiplicity of phenomena is also explained by the theory of the Receptacle, for phenomenal events occurring therein are many individual events that can be multiplied or divided even though each possesses a distinctive individuality. The Forms or Ideals, however, are simple, indivisible, and one. Whatever occurs in the world transpires within the Receptacle, for within it are generated phenomena that are in process, that live and move and have their being. Within the Receptacle, generated objects, that is, physical things, are continuously in a process of becoming.

As a container of events, the Receptacle accounts for the realm of existence, the arena in which the actual takes place. It is the matter-of-fact world. Within it brute matter (unformed substance) was taken by God, the Demiurge, and perpetually fashioned into the physical world as it is presently known. The Receptacle accounts for "passing things" rather than eternal entities. These passing things (generation), composed of matter-of-fact properties, acquire their structure and order from the Platonic Forms or Ideals (*paradeigma*). But without the Receptacle, the Ideal cannot make its transition to the actual; hence the Receptacle serves as the principle of existence. The more Form that is found embodied in phenomena (matter-of-fact existence), the greater its reality, perfection, goodness, maturity, formation, and actuality.

The Receptacle and the Factor of Necessity: The Explanation of the Problem of Natural Evil. To account for the presence of brute datum or surd matter, Plato introduced the factor of "necessity" (*anagkē*). The Greek word *anagkē* is commonly translated as force, necessity, or constraint. When God fashioned brute matter, he did so working under certain constraints, limitations, or handicaps. "Even God is said not to be able to fight against *necessity*."[3] Because matter had only a limited potential of being perfected, it was a necessity that God produced a world containing deficiencies. The deficiencies, however, are not due to God but to the character and limitations of the raw matter with which he had to cope. Brute data were the best that the Receptacle provided.

The current world is not pure Form (Idea) or surd, unfashioned matter, but a mixture of the prototype and brute datum. It is a generative process bent on perfection, despite its inability to achieve absolute perfection. Thus the world is in a state of being perfected. Explaining his position, Plato wrote that the efforts of intelligence must confront "the things which come into being through necessity—for the creation is mixed, being made up of necessity and mind. Mind, the ruling power, persuaded necessity to bring the greater part of created things to perfection, and thus and after this manner in the beginning, when the influence of reason got the better of necessity, the university was created."[4]

Anagkē ("necessity" or "constraint") is *the given*, and not what God created. It is the characteristic stuff of which the objects of sense experience are made. *Anagkē* comprises brute facts as God found them in the beginning, and is not material of his own choosing. In the mortal soul, observed Plato, the *anagkē* is found as part of human nature in the form of instinctual urges, compulsions, uncontrolled and irrational emotions, and compulsive impulses. They are brute facts of the given—the Receptacle and its factor of *anagkē*. The Receptacle and *anagkē* are factors "other" than (that is, in addition to) God; hence God is not regarded by Plato as an absolute creator. In the creation of the world there are factors coeternal with God. God does not create *ex nihilo* ("out of nothing") but fashions the world with the materials provided him as if he were an artisan.

Because the Receptacle accounts for Not-Being, the given, the surd, and brute fact, it is that aspect of the world which fails of necessary explanations and is explained in nonrational (if not irrational) terms, owing to inexplicable facts. For example, while mathematical and logical principles follow by necessity (for example, $2 + 2 = 4$; or, "any self-contradictory statement must be false"), brute facts are devoid of logical necessity. Thus there is no necessary reason why a human being is born with five fingers on each hand instead of six or four. Accordingly, paradoxical problems troubling the philosopher of religion arise from brute facts or the surd, that is, the given or Receptacle. What Plato is trying to say is that God did not create the world out of nothing, but was limited to the raw data, indeterminate plasticity, or formless, chaotic material provided him by the Receptacle. God created the world out of this sort of nothingness. Although the Ideals are perfect, the material world cannot be, for the physical world of nature was not made out of the same substance as the world of Ideals. The material provided to Plato's God by the Receptacle had inherent limitations, precluding any possibility of its ever becoming perfect. It is as though God were asked to make a silk purse out of a sow's ear. Or, better still, it is like asking God to make a perfect snowball and let it remain a year in a room temperature of one thousand degrees. Human engineers and scientists face the same problem with the surd or brute matter of

Plato's Receptacle. If you were to ask an engineer to make a perfect one-inch ball out of cement, he would say that it would be too rough to be considered a perfect inch. If you changed your request to a perfect one-inch steel ball, the engineer would ask for tolerances within which he would have to stay; that is, if you provided him with tolerances of 1/1000 of an inch, then he would have a margin of 2/1000 of an inch with which to play. Provided that he did not deviate from the tolerances specified, he would consider his ball perfect. But looking at such a ball through a microscope, one would find that the ball would be far from perfect; it would be completely undulated. If the observer then complained that the ball was not perfect enough, the engineer would announce that it was the best that could be done with the materials with which he was expected to work. The same holds true for God. If matter is innately and inherently imperfect, hence incapable of perfection, then the best that God can do is improve it depending on the potential the element possesses. If it is devoid of any potential for perfection, then God cannot make it completely perfect. Thus God perfects the world of existence by making it the best that is possible. Why did God bother in the first place to fashion the world if he knew that it is impossible to make it absolutely perfect? Plato's response is: Because it was good. Goodness is not only the reason for creating the world but, in addition, is the motivation and teleological goal of it as well.

The difficulty arises not because the Receptacle is opposed to God, but because it is "other" (another characteristic quality) than God. It is for this reason that the Receptacle (brute matter) resists God. Unlike logical and mathematical principles, the Receptacle lacks determinateness, and hence is indeterminate. But it is not completely irrational, as is evidenced by the reasons scientists provide for the explanation of phenomena, including rational explanations of abnormal psychological behavior. The reasons given, however, are not the same as the logical reasons based upon mathematical reasoning. Accordingly, Plato refers to reasoning dealing with matter-of-fact existence of the Receptacle as a "bastard" kind of reason. Comparing the three categories of the universe, namely, Being (Pattern or Ideals), Receptacle (space and brute matter), and Generation (phenomenal existence), Plato asserted:

We must acknowledge that there is one kind of Being which is always the same, uncreated and indestructible, . . . invisible and imperceptible by any sense, and of which the contemplation is granted to intelligence only. And there is another nature of the same name with it, and like to it, perceived by sense, created, always in motion, becoming in place and again vanishing out of place, which is apprehended by opinion and sense. And there is a third nature, which is Space, and is eternal, and admits not of destruction and provides a home for all created things, and is apprehended without the help of sense, by a kind of spurious reason, and is hardly real; which we beholding as in a dream, say of all existence that it must of necessity be in some place and occupy a space, but that what is neither in heaven nor in earth has no existence.[5]

Plato places dreams into the category of those things devoid of existence. Note that Plato regards space as known through a counterfeit type of reason rather than through sense perception. The Pattern, Receptacle, and Generation existed prior to heaven, that is, they are eternal, or coeternal with the Being of God. Furthermore, the Receptacle and the Pattern are external to God, rather than being part of his nature. Neither the Pattern nor the Receptacle were created by God. Time was a creation, but eternity was not a creation, because time is a process in the world of existence, while eternity transcends all time. Some Plato scholars, such as Raphael Demos, argue that the Receptacle "is not simply space, but space-time."[6] But this rendition seems to be due to the influence of contemporary philosophers who, like Samuel Alexander, argue that space does not exist without time and vice versa, and hence that space-time is a unitary notion. Plato unequivocally stated that the Receptacle is *apeirōn*, a boundless, endless space. This notion, it will be recalled by anyone who has studied the history of philosophy, reflects the influence of the philosopher Anaximander. The confusion arises from the fact that Plato identified the container of events as space *(chōra)* as well as the Receptacle *(dexamenē)*.

The Greek word *dexamenē*, translated by philosophers as Receptacle, means a receptacle for water, a reservoir, a cistern, or tank. Its secondary meaning, the Platonic one, means that which is capable of form, hence matter. Of the Receptacle, Plato explained:

That which is to receive all forms should have no form; as in making perfumes they first contrive that the liquid substance which is to receive the scent shall be as inodorous as possible. . . . In the same way that which is to receive perpetually and through its whole extent the resemblances of all eternal beings ought to be devoid of any particular form. Wherefore, the mother and Receptacle of all created and visible and in any way sensible things, is not to be termed earth, or air, or fire, or water, or any of their compounds or any of the elements from which these are derived, but is an invisible and formless Being which receives all things and in some mysterious way partakes of the intelligible, and is most incomprehensible.[7]

Earth, air, fire, and water, of which Plato spoke, constitute the basic chemical elements of which the physical world is composed. This elemental composition of the world Plato derived from the pre-Socratic philosopher Empedocles of Agrigentum, Sicily (495–435 B.C.).

Space is regarded as an entity though devoid of form yet capable of receiving any form; that is, it receives the impress of any of the Platonic Ideals. While the elements in the physical world are in constant flux, space has a nature that is permanently fixed. Space, according to Plato, is

the universal nature which receives all bodies that must always be called the same; for, while receiving all things, she never departs at all from her own nature, and never in any way, or at any time, assumes a form like that of any of the things which enter into her; she is the natural recipient of all impressions, and is stirred and informed by them, and appears different from time to time by reason of them. But the forms which enter into and go out of her are like likenesses of real existences modelled after their patterns in a wonderful and inexplicable manner. . . . We have only to conceive of three natures: first, that which is in process of Generation; secondly, that in which the Generation takes place [Receptacle]; and thirdly, that of which the thing Generated is a resemblance [Pattern or Ideal].[8]

Plato relegated time to the sphere of Becoming; hence it is one of the elements in Generation. Eternity, however, is not such an element; it is eternal, as are the other Ideal entities. Time, then, is an imitation of eternity, merely a copy of eternity. The original, prototype, or Pattern (that is, *paradeigma*) is eternity, time being its replica. The original of time is eternity. While eternity is Ideal Being, time is generated, that is, a creation. Explicating his theory of time, Plato asserted that the Creator

determined to make the copy still more like the original; and as this was eternal, he sought to make the universe eternal, so far as might be. Now the nature of the Ideal Being was everlasting, but to bestow this attribute in its fulness upon a creature was impossible. Wherefore he resolved to have a moving image of eternity . . . , he made this image eternal . . . ; and this image we call time. For there were no days and nights and months and years. . . . They are all parts of time, and the past and future are created species of time, which we unconsciously but wrongfully transfer to the eternal essence; for we say that he "was" he "is," he "will be," but the truth is that "is" alone is properly attributed to him, and that "was" and "will be" are only to be spoken of becoming in time, for they are motions, but that which is immoveably the same cannot become older or younger by time, nor ever did or has become, or hereafter will be, older or younger, nor is subject at all to any of those states which affect moving and sensible things and of which Generation is the cause. These are the Forms of time, which imitates eternity.[9]

Time, then, is the moving image or copy of eternity. The Ideals, as eternal essence, or substance (*ousia*), are immovable and eternal. While the Pattern of time exists from all eternity, time, a creation or phenomenon, strives toward perfection by seeking to press on toward whatever immortality lies within its capability. The modes of time, unlike its eternal essence, cannot be regarded as modes continuing through everlasting stages.

The heavens, created with the inception of time, will endure as long as time lasts.

Time, then, and the heaven came into being at the same instant in order that, having been created together, if ever there was to be a dissolution of them, they might be dissolved together. It was framed after the pattern of the eternal nature, that it might resemble this as far as was possible; for the Pattern exists from eternity, and the created heaven has been, and is, and will be, in all time.[10]

God had this thought in mind when he created time.

Generation: The Actual or Created World. The world in the process of Becoming, that is, the actual or phenomenal world undergoing its evolutionary process, Plato called the world of Generation (*genesis*). The Greek word *genesis* literally means production, generation, birth, origin, source, or productive cause. Plato's use of the term is best appreciated in the *Philebus*, where he quotes the following inquiry by Socrates: "Is not destruction universally admitted to be the opposite of generation?"[11] Hence the generated world is the ongoing process that has undergone a beginning at some point in time.

Generation is the world we observe with our senses, occurring in some temporal sequence; it is the phenomenal world developing in space and in time. It is the world of perception as opposed to the world of conception. It is the world of things rather than the world of thought. It is the actual rather than the ideal world. It is the world God created rather than his conception of it before he began. It is the temporal rather than the eternal world. It is a copy of the ultimate, the ontologically real world. It is a world coming into being (the world of Becoming), not the world of Being. It is the world perfecting itself, not the perfect world (Ideal world).

Despite the foregoing differences between the two worlds of Plato, the actual and the Ideal, the two are not that sharply dichotomized, for the actual world is a mixture of the Receptacle and the Ideal. Surd or brute matter, it will be remembered, was characteristic of the Receptacle. The actual or world of Generation, however, is a mixture of the two. Plato depicted the Pattern (world of Ideas) as siring this world, the Receptacle as mothering it, and their offspring as the world of Becoming (*genesis*). Thus, whereas Being is the father, and Receptacle the mother, the world of Generation is the child. "We may liken the receiving principle to a mother," asserted Plato, "and the source or spring to a father, and the intermediate nature to a child."[12] Just as people speak of mother earth, Plato speaks of the mother Receptacle.

Plato is not a materialist but an idealist; his belief is that Ideals are real. When philosophers refer to him as a realist, they do not mean that Plato regarded material objects as real but that he thought Ideals to be real. The Platonic theory that Ideals are real makes him an idealist by virtue of his belief in Ideals, and also a realist by virtue of his belief in a genuinely real substance, namely, Ideals.

The term "matter" owes its increased application in the history of philosophy to Aristotle, not to Plato. Plato rarely made use of the term. Matter (*materia*) is actually a Latin derivative. Its Greek counterpart, the term employed chiefly by Aristotle, is *hylē*, meaning wood or woodland. It later acquired the meaning of "matter" or "stuff" of which things are made, that is, the raw unwrought material—the material could be either wood or subject matter for a poem. An ultimate reality, the source of Being, it was used by Aristotle, and especially by subsequent philosophers who used it in contradistinction to mind, especially in opposition to the concept of *nous*, mind as the intelligent principle. Although philosophers occasionally employ the word matter (*hylē*) in speaking of Plato's surd or brute "matter," many of them strive to avoid use of the term since the term matter *(hylē)*, the "unformed stuff" of Aristotle, had not yet acquired this connotation for Plato.

Accordingly, Plato's Generation *(genesis)* is not a material thing; it is not stuff or matter *(hylē)*. What then is it? Rather than being a static thing, it is a developmental process, a mixture of the Ideals (Patterns) and Receptacle that he termed Becoming or Generation. A horse, for example, is neither static nor material, but a dynamic process in continuous development toward perfection. Tragically, objects perish before attaining ideal perfection. But the more the Ideal is infused into created or generated things, the closer they will approximate perfection.

Plato spoke of this union of the Ideal Pattern with phenomena or Generation as "participation," "imitation," and "partaking" of the sensed copy with the supersensible Ideal or prototype. Thus the world of perception strives to emulate the world of conception. Plato quoted Socrates' claim that "there are certain ideas of which all other things partake, and from which they derive their names; that similars, for example, become similar, because they partake of similarity; and great things become great, because they partake of greatness; and that just and beautiful things become just and beautiful, because they partake of justice and beauty."[13] The more the Ideal cohabits with the phenomenal things, the more the generated object acquires the property or characteristics of the Ideal. Consequently, a thing is beautiful because the Ideal of beauty shines through it in a participatory relationship.

III *Immortality of the Soul*

Plato assigned the human soul an intermediary position between the world of Becoming (Generation) and the world of Ideal Being. Whereas the former was created in time and perished, the latter was timeless or eternal, hence immutable. While the soul is not eternal, it is nevertheless by its very nature immortal. Although the soul had a beginning, its existence is endless. To be eternal is to be outside of time, to transcend it, whereas to be immortal is to live as long as time lasts.

Unlike physical things, the soul survives change. Since the soul's quintessence is life, it cannot be in a state of death. Rather than belonging to the dimension of Generation, the soul's domain is the supersensible world. Notwithstanding its dwelling in the world of Generation, the soul is similar to (but not identical with) Ideals. As the carrier of the Idea of life, the soul is not only immortal but has enjoyed a preexistence, a life prior to its earthly one; we have here, then, a doctrine of the transmigration of souls.

It is, however, the intellective or rational soul that is everlasting, not the mortal soul which finds its abode in the breast and the thorax. More will be said of the mortal soul later; suffice it to say here that its two constituent aspects consist of the seats of passion and of desire. The immortal soul, whose locus is the head, is the only one which can be properly identified as a mind, the only one which possesses the capacity of reason and intellect.

While Plato is opposed to suicide, he does maintain a belief in the blessedness of death, because it is only under that circumstance that the "greatest good" is within a person's grasp. The true philosopher is always dying, because he is constantly striving to attain the world of Ideals, despite the inhibitions of the body and its attending evils. A prisoner of the body, the philosopher regards death as merely the separation of body and soul, the freeing of the soul. Moments before the death of Socrates, Plato recorded his mentor's convictions:

I have reason to prove to you that the real philosopher has reason to be of good cheer when he is about to die, and that after death he may hope to obtain the greatest good in the other world. . . . He is always pursuing death and dying. . . .

Is it not the separation of soul and body? And to be dead is the completion of this; when the soul exists in herself, and is released from the body and the body is released from the soul, what is this but death? . . . He would like, as far as he can, to get away from the body and to turn to the soul. . . .

Then when does the soul attain truth?—for in attempting to consider anything in company with the body she is obviously deceived. . . .

Then must not true existence be revealed to her in thought, if at all?

And thought is best when the mind is gathered into herself and none of these things trouble her—neither sounds nor sights nor pain. . . .

True philosophers, and they only, are ever seeking to release the soul. . . .

True philosophers . . . are always occupied in the practice of dying. . . .

When you see a man who is repining at the approach of death, is not his reluctance a sufficient proof that he is not a lover of wisdom, but a lover of the body.[14]

Some of the ideas expressed in the above quotation fructified into the Manichaeanism of the third and fourth centuries in Rome. This is particularly true regarding its relegation of flesh to the realm of darkness and its concomitant doctrine of asceticism.

IV   *God: The Demiurge*

The two principal words that Plato employs when referring to the supreme God are *theos* and *dēmiourgos*. Theology, the study of God, derives from the former term. The New Testament uses the same term for the Christian God, except that it is accompanied by the definite article "the." It is the second term for God (*dēmiourgos*), however, that came to characterize Plato's God, the creator of the physical or phenomenal world in accord with the eternal Ideas. The Greek term *dēmiourgos* means literally "a worker for the people"; it may also be translated as a "skilled workman" or "handicraftsman," and even a "maker," "framer," or "author." For Plato, the Demiurge was the maker of the world, its fashioner, artificer, or designer, hence creator.

In the *Republic*, Plato rhetorically asked: "Will he [the astronomer] not think that heaven and the things in heaven are framed by the Creator of them in the most perfect manner?"[15] In the *Timaeus*, Plato explained: "Thus far and until the birth of time the created universe was made in the likeness of the original, but inasmuch as all animals were not yet comprehended therein, it was still unlike. What remained, the Creator then proceeded to fashion after the nature of the Pattern."[16] Later Plato added, "I am the Artificer and father, my creations are indissoluble, if so I will."[17]

Lacking omnipotence, Plato's God, rather than bending the world to his will by fiat, emerged as a moral force. God is neither infinite nor an absolute creator. With limitations placed upon his power, God is but one of a number of factors accounting for the universe. His principal role is as the necessary principle accounting for the relatedness of the Idea (Pattern) to the Receptacle. In this sense God is the Creator or the cause, while the phenomenal world in development is the effect of God's activity. Hence, the world of Generation, the world of Becoming, depends upon God. Because God has willed it, the world endures.

God is not the only ultimate or factor necessary in bringing about the universe, for factors other than God include the Ideal and the

Receptacle, each of which is eternal, hence uncreated. God is contrasted to the Receptacle as teleology is to brute datum or fact. The
creative factors are contrasted to the created as the transcendental is
to the phenomenal world.

Although Plato's God is impersonal rather than a person, he is not
only morally perfect but engages in moral conflicts. Furthermore,
he expresses a loving care for his creation. Thus his nature is one of
goodness. In fact, so good is Plato's God that some scholars characterize him as the Idea of the good—which if not literally the case,
then at least allegorically.

God is the efficient cause of the generated world (nature), and is
regarded by Plato as "the mover," and occasionally as "the moved."
God has not only brought the world into being (toward Ideal Being),
but has fashioned it also, hence is both the maker of nature and its
designer, as well as its purposive cause. God, as the maker of the
temporal world, is himself ungenerated and timeless. God is intelligent creativity, as the following Platonic dialogue from the *Sophist*
(concerning the natural world as imitation of the Ideal) testifies:

Imitation is a kind of creation—of images, however, as we affirm, and not of
real things [Ideas]. . . .

Looking, now, at the world and all the animals and plants, as at inanimate
substances which are formed within the earth, fusile or non-fusile, shall we
say that they come into existence—not having existed previously—by the
creation of God, or shall we agree with vulgar opinion about them?

What is it?

The opinion that nature brings them into being from some spontaneous
and unintelligent cause. Or shall we say that they are created by a divine
reason and a knowledge which comes from God?[18]

The answer supplied by Plato, was to be sure, that an intelligent
God was responsible for creation. God, as the maker of the world,
rendered it intelligible through the operation of divine reason in the
world and rendered it purposeful by virtue of the good.

The polytheism that was prevalent in Plato's time made somewhat
of an appearance in Plato's philosophy of religion. Unlike the supreme God that we have been discussing, the lesser gods are
created. As natural forces, they serve as adjuncts to God, while God
transcends natural forces as their creator. Furthermore, as creator of
the temporal world, God is morally perfect, but these lesser or
created divinities serve to explain the evil as well as the good forces

pervading nature. There are also morally indifferent gods whose function is the originating or generating of motion. While the lesser gods became involved in the subordinate or perishable aspects of the world, the supreme God dealt with its superior or immortal dimension. Plato asserted that the part "worthy of the name immortal, which is called divine and is the guiding principle of those who are willing to follow justice and you—of that divine part I will my self sow the seed."[19] Thus, the best the created world has to offer is in God's care and control, leaving the lesser and questionable portion to the created gods or forces of nature. Like human beings the created gods are immortal, but not eternal. God, being timeless, is eternal. But the created gods, because they exist in time, are temporal. Unlike God, pure and simple, the created gods are mixtures, impure, and partake of the world's unruly character, for in addition to gods there are demons. Unlike the real God, the created gods are not absolutely real nor are they absolutely good. "God is not the author of all things," declared Plato, "but of good only."[20] Furthermore, since "God and the things of God are in every way perfect," it follows that "it is impossible that God should ever be willing to change, being . . . the fairest and best that is conceivable."[21] Hence we have the immutable nature of God, as well as an absolutely good God. Inasmuch as God is not the cause of all things, yet is absolutely good, he is not held accountable for evil. Consequently, in order to preserve God's goodness, Plato was obliged to limit God's omnipotence.

Since the presence of evil in the world is not of God's doing, how then does Plato resolve the problem? Although some of it was imputed to the lesser gods, that is not an adequate explanation, since the gods are created.

Plato's major explanation is in terms of the given, the brute matter provided God in the Receptacle. This notion, discussed earlier in this chapter, explained evil as a limitation or necessity (*anagkē*). The raw material with which God had to fashion the world was made of an element that was incapable of absolute perfection. This temporal world, then, is the best that could be created under the circumstances. Despite its deficiencies, it was deemed better by God to proceed with constructing the world than not to go ahead with the project. Accordingly, God's criterion in determining whether or not to act is goodness rather than perfection. Goodness not only motivates God, but also motivates the entire world. Although God's omnipotence is not absolute—since he could not effect the perfect universe that he would prefer—his goodness is absolute. In sum, the errant Receptacle with its chaotic nature is the cause of evil. Therefore, only the temporal world is caught in the throes of evil.

Dispensing with evil because of its unreal status, Plato held that to the degree that an object is unreal, to that extent it is evil. Consequently, evil lacks reality.

V *Concluding Comments*

To ponder why the penetrating mind of Plato would be reduced to entertaining polytheism in such a sophisticated system of philosophy is understandable. But it is equally understandable why he did. His philosophy was shaped by contemporary influences— polytheism was at its height. Yet, as the active and thoughtful mind of Plato wrestled with philosophical ideas, he tended to reject the polytheism of the Greeks out of preference for monotheism, in which one spiritual God figured as a father God and a shepherd of his creation rather than as a demiurge and artificer. Whereas the earlier Plato had us understand that the Ideas and prototypes were the causes of the phenomenal world (temporal world of Generation), the later Plato has us believe that they (in and of themselves) are insufficient to explain the temporal world. Accordingly, God becomes an important hypothesis.

Nevertheless, Plato does not adduce arguments for the existence of God. Rather, he relegates the issue to a matter of personal religious experience; so regarded, it becomes a private affair.

Although Moses was a thirteenth-century B.C. figure, and Plato lived many centuries later, there are many striking resemblances in their religious philosophies. So similar are they that some scholars feel that research should be conducted with respect to these two thinkers in order to ascertain whether or not one was privy to the sources or philosophy of the other.

CHAPTER 8

Epistemology and Metaphysics: Plato's Twofold Theory of Knowledge and Reality

THE English language can scarcely do justice to the brilliance and profundity of Plato's mind; but he was nevertheless a child of his age. He drew heavily not only from Socratic philosophy but also from the great philosophers who preceded him. In a very real sense Plato synthesized a number of earlier philosophies, the happy consequences being Platonic epistemology (theory of knowledge) and Platonic metaphysics (theory of reality).

What Plato confronted and what Plato sought to reconcile were the divergent philosophies of his predecessors, philosophies that to him were quite meaningful and cogent. A distinguished Sophist, Protagoras, had successfully established (at least to Plato's satisfaction) that our sense perceptions never provide us with absolute truth, unchanging reality, or scientific knowledge, but merely with relative truths. This, it was reasoned, was due to reality being in a state of process or change, resulting in a cluster of shifting opinions instead of everlasting and immutable facts. Socrates, in opposition to Protagoras, argued for a permanent character in reality; he therefore regarded truth as consisting of unchanging essences. Because knowledge is scientifically sound, it transcends opinion and relativity; hence, it is a carefully reasoned opinion. Plato also found himself in accord with the Socratic position. On these two apparently disparate epistemologies, Plato predicated his theory of knowledge.

The second major reconciliation undertaken by Plato concerned two diverse kinds of reality: on the one hand, the Heraclitian flux, a world of constant change or Becoming, thus a perpetual process; on the other hand, the view of Parmenides that the universe is one permanent Being and is therefore primordial and immutable. Plato adopted both views, referring to Heraclitian flux or Becoming as

145

"phenomena," and to Parmenidian "Being" as noumenal, ideal, or ontological reality. The imitation of Being by Becoming was a concept Plato derived from Pythagoras, according to Aristotle, but Plato termed the imitation of the Forms or Ideas "participation."

The two problems or issues, epistemological dualism and metaphysical dualism, are not to be regarded as separate or isolated issues, for they are interrelated. A person's epistemology determines his metaphysical position. An epistemology that is based on changing perceptions results in a metaphysics of Becoming, whereas an epistemology that is predicated on universal concepts yields a permanent *uni*verse, a single reality or Being that is not subject to perpetual change. Let us examine these two epistemologies and metaphysics in detail together with the ramifications they hold for contemporary science and everyday living.

I   *Plato's Dialectic*

The Greek term dialectic *(dialektikos)*, derived from discourse, dialogue, conversation, connotes a debate, discussion, or argument. The art of dialectic, which was introduced by Zeno of Elea and perfected by Socrates, is the technique of deliberating on philosophical issues by raising questions and seeking answers to them, with the prospect that truth may evolve through such dialogue. In one sense, dialectic is a logical debate.

Plato's use of dialectic had a dual significance. One aspect is the Socratic technique of philosophical discourse, that is, a technique for presenting philosophical views in the form of a dialogue, such as found in virtually all of his writings on philosophy. The dialogue, however, is undertaken by an individual called the dialectician (usually Socrates) raising questions and the respondent providing answers. The answers are challenged if terms are ill-defined or if an adequate account or logical explanation is not provided. Hopefully, by this technique knowledge of Platonic Ideals is realized. A second aspect of the term, a methodological and epistemological one, is the immediate apprehension of Platonic Ideas. It is, therefore, a form of knowing, as distinguished from imagining, believing, or even thinking. Some scholars even identify the dialectic with Plato's theory of Ideas; at least the knowledge of them is acquired through the dialectic.

The art of dialectic, the technique of effecting truth through philosophical discussion, is well illustrated by Socrates in the following dialogue with Hermogenes:

SOCRATES. And who uses the work of the lyre-maker? Will not he be the man who knows how to direct what is being done, and who will know also whether the work is being well done or not?
HERMOGENES. Certainly.
SOCRATES. And who is he?
HERMOGENES. The player of the lyre.
SOCRATES. And who will direct the shipwright?
HERMOGENES. The pilot.
SOCRATES. And who will be best able to direct the legislator in his work, and will know whether the work is well done, in this or any other country? Will not the user be the man?
HERMOGENES. Yes.
SOCRATES. And this is he who knows how to ask questions?
HERMOGENES. Yes.
SOCRATES. And how to answer them?
HERMOGENES. Yes.
SOCRATES. And he who knows how to ask and answer you would be called a dialectician?
HERMOGENES. Yes.
SOCRATES. Then the work of the carpenter is to make a rudder, and the pilot has to direct him, if the rudder is to be well made?
HERMOGENES. Yes.
SOCRATES. And the work of the legislator is to give names, and the dialectician must be his director if the names are to be rightly given. . . .[1]

Scholars have noted that dialectic has acquired a number of connotations with Plato, including the ideal method, the upward path of knowledge superseding the hypothetical method of mathematics, the method of synthesis, and the method of division. Invariably it included the search for reality *(ousia,* that is, substance or essence), that which abides or remains the same when other characteristics of an object come into existence and pass away. The advancement of knowledge is, therefore, dialectic.

Whereas for Socrates dialectic was reasoning conducted through dialogue as a technique of intellectual investigation, for Plato it was a method for investigating ontological reality, that is, the Ideal world or the world of true Being. By it he meant the ability to go beyond the limitations of sense perception directly to the world of ultimate reality, the Platonic transcendental realm of Ideal Being in contrast to the perceptual or phenomenal world as it appears to us through our senses. Just as the purpose of sense organs is to observe the sense world, so the purpose of the dialectic is to make contact with the realm of the absolute, the ideal world. Plato elaborated:

This is that strain which is of the intellect only, but which the faculty of sight will nevertheless be found to imitate. . . . And so with the dialectic; when a person starts on the discovery of the absolute by the light of reason only, and without any assistance of sense, and perseveres until by pure intelligence he arrives at the perception of the absolute good, he at last finds himself at the end of the intellectual world, as in the case of sight at the end of the whole.[2]

Thus, the dialectic is that method by which the Platonic Ideals are discerned and known. We shall return to the Platonic world of Ideas later, but suffice it to say at this point that knowledge which is absolutely true and enduring derives from the dialectic. As such, it is knowledge stemming from first principles and ultimately from the Platonic Idea of the Good. The Good itself is known by the dialectic. Dialectical intellection entails immediate and rational intuition or direct apprehension rather than discursive reasoning or hypothetical reasoning. That is to say, one's mind makes contact directly with Platonic Ideals and the Good or it does not, because the Good transcends all rational deliberation. Either one intuits the Good or it remains an unknown enigma, an unknown entity, as if one were a subhuman creature.

Plato arranged the various mental states of cognitive activity in ascending order as: (1) imagining, (2) believing, (3) thinking, and (4) dialectical cognizing (knowing). The latter two, classified under intellection, were considered superior to the first two, which were nonrational forms of cognition that Plato classified under the cognitive activity of opining. Plato explained by calling

the first division dialectical knowledge, the second thinking, the third belief, and the fourth imagery or picture thought—and the last two collectively opinion, and the first two intellection, opinion dealing with the apprehension of appearances in the world of Becoming, and intellection with true Being. As Being is to Becoming, so is intellection to opinion; and as intellection is to opinion, so is science to belief, and thinking to imagining [phantasizing or picture thought].[3]

The accompanying table or schematic can help to clarify Plato's division of mental states of cognition. Each succeeding stage of cognitive activity brings one closer to reality from mere conjecture, *epistēmē* ("scientific knowing") being the superlative form of human knowing.

Imagining, Picturing, or Fantasizing (Eikasia). The most naive form of knowing, *eikasia*, transpires in the world of imagination, the sphere of illusion, or what Plato identified in his allegory of the cave as *shadows* of reality. Accordingly, we are dealing with a subjective world that is at best a personal opinion or shadowy reality.

As the lowest stage of cognizing, *eikasia* (a term that defies definition) provides but the shallowest kind of knowledge or contact with reality. Although the usual meaning of the Greek word *eikasia* is "conjecture," Plato resorted to its etymological roots for the notion he gave it. Etymologically, it is related to *eikon*, meaning image, copy, or likeness; and to *eikos*, meaning like the truth. Hence, it can also be rendered as representation or conjecture. Imagining or fantasizing come closer to Plato's sense of the word, *eikasia*, although translators have rendered it image thinking, picturing, perception of shadows, conjecture, picture thought, imagining, mirroring (such as reflections on water), and the like.

Rather than providing us with realities of the world, *eikasia* furnishes us with mere reflections, images, or shadows of reality at best. Plato resorted to the allegory of the cave to depict cognizing at this most unsophisticated level of grasping the world. This mode of cognizing activity is characterized by imagining, fantasizing, conjecturing, or picturing the world mentally. While some states of *eikasia* are devoid of truth, other states do contain some. *Eikasia*, as cognizing, deals with iconic representation, the type of thinking that transpires when a person asks: "Would you like me to draw a picture for you?" Plato placed the fine arts in this category.

Belief (Pistis). The second stage of moving closer to reality is via belief, faith, conviction *(pistis)*. The movement is away from the world of shadows, of illusion, by establishing sense contact with the tangible world. While the world of shadows, of illusion, is intangible, the phenomenal world of sense objects can be touched, tasted, smelled, seen, and heard. Establishing contact with the sensate world heightens a person's belief or faith in the outer world. Accordingly, one has more of a feeling of certainty when he actually makes contact with objects of perception than with the merely mental images he finds in his world of dreams, reveries, or fantasy. As a consequence, a person's opinions are much firmer when based on *pistis* or sense perception than upon *eikasia* or the wild play of imagination.

Both *pistis* and *eikasia* are classed by Plato as nonrational activities of the mind that produce opinion rather than knowledge. While a person's opinion might prove to be quite correct, it does not become genuine knowledge until it is rationally accounted for by some adequate explanation.

Because cognitive dissonance arises in the mind, owing to contradictions arising from the sensate world, an individual is driven to look for other means of ascertaining truth. No longer does the mind seek for this truth in sense objects that are undergoing continuous change; instead, it is sought in the essence of the object that defies change, that is, the law which governs phenomena that Plato termed "Form." To obtain the object's essence or Form, rational cognitive activity is required, hence one must leave behind opining as the channel of cognitive activity and turn to intellection. Plato cited two forms of cognizing by intellection: thinking or understanding; and the highest degree of sophistication, dialectical knowledge or intuitive thought.

Thinking (Dianoia). In shifting from Class I (opining) to Class II (intellection), cognizing moves from the observable to the invisible, from images to symbols, from perception to conception, from sense to thought. Instead of being concerned with particular events or objects, one is now interested in universal laws or the essence of the object, that is, in what a particular object shares with all other objects of its kind. For example, one shifts attention from a particular person who happens to be one's father to human beings in general, that is, from the individual to humanity. While the former are phenomenal objects, the latter are Platonic Forms, Ideas, or Patterns.

Thinking *(dianoia)*, then, is dealing with symbols as in mathematics, symbolic logic, and principles rather than with particular empirical objects. Objects of thought supersede objects of sense. One leaves the realm of sense for the domain of science. While triangularity is a rational thought, a particular triangle observed by the sense of sight is not; it is merely a perception of one and lacks the perfection of the Ideal, its prototype.

By *dianoia* ("thinking"), Plato had in mind deductive reasoning, hypothetical reasoning, or that found in mathematical reasoning. To Plato, these three forms of reasoning are equivalent or identical. Geometrical or arithmetical reasoning is predicated on certain assumptions or hypotheses, from which one must reason consistently to a conclusion. The hypothetical basis of mathematics rests on an assumption (axioms, postulates, etc.); if this hypothetical base is not granted then no valid conclusions can follow. Accordingly, for Plato, an hypothesis is an assumed truth taken as primary or ultimate when actually it is contingent upon a still higher truth. However, this does not mean that hypothetical truths are or can be proved false. Without axioms, postulates, and definitions, reasoning is critically hampered. Every science rests on its hypotheses, that is, on its axiomatic truths which are accepted as self-evident, and are, accordingly, not proved. They await confirmation by being interconnected with the whole, with the body of knowledge conceived of as a systematic whole. But to attain a systematic whole, perfect knowledge, it is necessary to relate all things to an unconditional principle upon which they are contingent. For ideal knowledge of this character, one must look to *epistēmē* ("dialectical knowledge" or "intuitive thought," the final stage and ultimate form of knowing or intellection).

Dialectical Knowing (Epistēmē). Dialectical knowing, which is intelligence in its perfection, is devoid of sense content. As the final stage of intellection, dialectical knowledge involves grasping all branches of knowledge synoptically *(synoptikos).* It is the viewing of all sciences as one unified science together with all other knowledge. As perfect knowledge, dialectical knowing depends upon the ability to comprehend the relationships of all elements of knowledge. Consequently, advancement in knowledge hinges upon progress in the apprehension of the unity of knowledge. Thus, dialectical knowledge is what knowing would be if our knowledge were perfect.

Hypotheses are no longer required in perfect intellection or dialectical knowledge. In the dialectic, the intellect transcends "hypothesis, and goes up to a principle which is above hypotheses, making no use of images . . . but proceeding only in and through the ideas themselves."[4] Explaining how the dialectic supersedes hypothetical reasoning, Plato pointed out that the dialectic utilizes the hypotheses not as first principles, but only as hypotheses—that is to say, as steps and points of departure into a world which is above hypotheses, in order that "she may soar beyond them to the first principle of the whole; and . . . by successive steps she descends again without the aid of any sensible object, from ideas, through ideas, and in ideas, she ends."[5] So, it is by the dialectic that one reaches the Good, Plato's one unconditioned principle, the principle upon which everything else in the universe is contingent. This principle upon which everything depends is the Good, the supreme and ultimate purpose of the world and its coming into existence. Thus it is that through perfect knowledge one arrives at perfect reality and the ultimate, Good. Just as perfect reality is an ideal, so is perfect knowledge. Just as the element of sense is absent in Ideal reality, so it is also absent in perfect intellection or perfect knowledge. Not only does one arrive at the Good through knowledge, but the Platonic Idea, Good, is the source of knowledge as well as knowability and also serves to account for the world of Ideas. Consequently, Ideas are not only known owing to their relation to the Good, but exist by virtue of the Idea of the Good. Even the virtues acquire their value and definition by their relation to the Good, life's *summum bonum*. Wisdom is the knowledge of Good, whereas courage, temperance, and justice serve in the pursuit of it. Virtues acquire excellence by their being good. When Plato speaks of God as the Good, he does not mean that God is identical with the Good, but that he too, like the virtues, is one of a number of good entities.

The Platonic Ideas (Forms, prototypes, archetypes, or Patterns—they are interchangeable terms) are mathematical and logical ways in which contemporary scientists view and deal with the phenomenal data of human experience. The Ideas or Forms of Plato are comparable to the formulas of scientists, to the scientists' mathematical and logical formulations of data in terms of equations and principles.

What Plato is trying to tell us is that the world of knowledge truly exists. In fact, it is the genuinely real one, whereas the world with which our senses make contact only *seems* to appear ultimate. The intelligible world has a greater degree of reality and truth than the visible world. While philosophers are lovers of Ideals (reality, truth, and wisdom), the untutored are lovers of appearance (conventional notions of the *hoi polloi* or common people).

In contemporary science, laws are derived from observations of the phenomenal world of sense and by experimentation (controlled observation of phenomena), whereas the Platonic approach called

WORLD OF REALITY or ULTIMATE BEING
(Noumena)
(Essence of Reality)
(Intelligible World)

DEGREES OF COGNITIVE STATES OR FUNCTIONS
(from the lowest to the highest form of knowing)

II. Cognizing by Intellection (*noēsis*)
(rational cognitive activity)

3. Thinking or Understanding (*dianoia*)
(Deductive reasoning; for example, discursive, hypothetical, or mathematical reasoning)

Object: Mathematical Entities

4. Dialectical Knowing (*epistēmē*)
(Synthetic reasoning; intuitive thought)

Object: Ideal Forms

I. Cognizing by Opining (*doxa*; opinion)
(nonrational cognitive activity)

1. Imagining (*eikasia*)
(Conjecture, picture thought; for example, picturing or fantasizing)

Object: Mental Images (devoid of an object of sense perception)

2. Believing (*pistis*)
(Faith; Conviction)
(for example, beliefs even correct ones, without knowledge)

Object: Objects of Perception

(Phenomena)
(Shadow of Reality)
(Visible World)

WORLD OF APPEARANCE or WORLD OF BECOMING

for the fastest possible exit from the world of appearances in order
not to confuse them with real entities. The body and its sense contacts with the visible world can be an impediment to the attainment
of knowledge of reality. It is the source of human confusion. From
the Platonic viewpoint the disembodied spirit devoid of sense interference might be in a better situation to acquire mathematical
knowledge. Factual information, historical data, and the like are
pseudoforms of knowledge and science.

II *The Duality of Knowledge and Reality*

If the reader will bear in mind Plato's conviction that two fundamental types of knowledge existed, each corresponding to a kind of
reality appropriate to it, it will be easier for him to appreciate the
Platonic theory of knowledge and reality. While perception apprehends a changing reality, thought grasps a durable reality. Thus
there are two types of cognition with its corresponding realm or
dimension of reality. Perception and its ever changing reality result
in a theory of truth as relative; thought, on the other hand, in
cognizing a lasting reality, yields a theory of truth as absolute.

Truth as Relative. The doctrine of the relativity of truth was
epitomized by the Protagorean dictum: "Man is the measure of all
things, of the existence of things that are, and of the non-existence of
things that are not."[6] That is to say, truth is relative to the person
uttering a statement. Truth, then, is simply a matter of opinion,
custom, or taste. What is true for you is true for you, and what is
true for me is true for me. Protagoras' classic declaration of this
doctrine reads: "Man is the measure of all things, and that things are
to me as they appear to me, and that they are to you as they appear
to you."[7] This theory did not originate with Protagoras, for it was
fostered by a number of the pre-Socratic philosophers, including
Heraclitus, Empedocles, and Democritus. It seems that the Eleatic
philosophers, spearheaded by Parmenides, were the chief opponents of this viewpoint. If these philosophers (Heraclitus, etc.) did
not actively support the relativity of truth theory, they did nevertheless indirectly lend credence to it by their philosophical stance.

One of the staunchest opponents to metaphysical and epistemological relativism, Socrates, defined the position accordingly:

I am about to speak of an illustrious philosophy, in which all things are said to be relative; you cannot rightly call anything by any name, such as great or small, or heavy or light, for the great will be small and the heavy light,—there is no one or some or any sort of nature, but out of motion and change and admixture all things are becoming, which "becoming" is by us incorrectly called being, but is really becoming, for nothing really is, but all things are becoming. Summon all philosophers,—Protagoras, Heraclitus, Empedocles, and the rest of them, one after another, with the exception of Parmenides, and they will agree with you in this. . . . All things are the offspring of flux.[8]

Although Heraclitus (fl. 505 B.C.) held reason to be the guide of all things, he did believe that "all things flow; nothing abides."[9] Inasmuch as there is no abiding reality, there can be no absolute truth or knowledge. Hence truth is relative. Reality is depicted as fire, ever changing, never abiding. A homogeneous, permanent, or absolute reality is out of the question. Reality is pictured as a flowing river that is never the same at any given moment owing to fresh waters entering it and water at the other end leaving it for the open sea. Consequently, "one cannot step twice into the same river,"[10] asserted Heraclitus. Plato, obviously considerably influenced by the Heraclitian philosophy, was also well tutored in it. Evidence of his Heraclitian bent is prevalent in his *Cratylus*, especially in such passages as the following: "Heraclitus is supposed to say that all things are in motion and nothing at rest; he compares them to the stream of a river, and says that you cannot go into the same water twice."[11] Earlier Plato made mention of those who "have inclined to the opinion of Heraclitus, that all things flow and nothing stands."[12]

Protagorean relativity stems from the fact that each individual possesses perceptions derived from his own private experiences. Inasmuch as no two people have the same experiences, no two can have exactly the same truth. Truth must, therefore, be relative. "My perception is true to me," argued Protagoras, "to myself I am judge of what is and what is not."[13]

Quite dissatisfied with Protagorean relativity, Socrates, with his characteristic irony, refuted it as follows:

I say nothing against his doctrine, that what appears is to each one, but I wonder that he did not begin his great work on Truth with a declaration that a pig or a dog-faced baboon, or some other stranger monster which has sensation, is the measure of all things; then, when we were reverencing him as a god, he might have condescended to inform us that he was no wiser than a tadpole and did not even aspire to be a man—would not this have produced an overpowering effect? For if truth is only sensation, and one man's discernment is as good as another's, and no man has any superior right to determine whether the opinion of any other is true or false, but each man . . . is to himself the sole judge, and everything that he judges is true and right, why should Protagoras be preferred to the place of wisdom and instruction, and deserve to be well paid, and we poor ignoramuses have to go to him, if each one is the measure of his own wisdom? . . . The attempt to supervise or refute the notions or opinions of others would be a tedious and enormous piece of folly, if to each man they are equally right; and this must be the case if Protagoras' Truth is the real truth, and if the philosopher is not merely amusing himself.[14]

Plato realized that the relativity of truth is a self-defeating doctrine, because anyone who is its votary is obliged to accept his opponent's position as valid despite its contradicting one's own theory. Plato, again placing his argument in the mouth of Socrates, laughingly wrote: "The best of the joke is, that he [Protagoras] acknowledges the truth of their opinion who believe his opinion to be false; for in admitting that the opinions of all men are true, in effect he grants that the opinion of his opponents is true. . . . And does he not allow that his own opinion is false, if he admits that the opinion of those who think him false is true?"[15]

In making the Protagorean premise appear ludicrous, Plato more than ridiculed Protagoras; he demolished the doctrine of the relativity of truth by an *ad absurdum* argument. A fairly common form of argument among the early Greek philosophers, the *argumentum ad absurdum* holds a position to be false when its premises yield contradictory or absurd conclusions.

Nevertheless, Plato did find a place for the doctrine of relativity in his philosophy. Opinion does play a role in the Platonic scheme, despite its not being classed as knowledge. Knowledge, as Plato viewed it, is conceptual understanding, comparable to what moderns think of as scientific theory. Opinion is grounded in our perceptions, but perceptions do not sense the ultimate or ontologically real, but the world as it *seems* to be. Rather, perceptions establish a contact between us and the phenomenal world—the sense world or the world as sensed. The term *phenomena* ("appearances," "manifestations"), which plays an important role in Platonic philosophy, was not new, for the term had been introduced by the Greek philosopher Democritus (ca. 460–360 B.C.). Plato relegated phenomena to the realm of generation *(genesis)* rather than to the eternal world of ultimate or ontological reality *(ontos* or *ousia),* the world of genuine Being.

Valid Knowledge: Truth as Absolute. Plato was well aware that science would be impossible if facts were in a state of constant change, without sharing any common characteristics. Scientific knowledge (both mathematical formula and scientific prediction) depends upon facts sharing behavioral traits as well as other uniform features, for otherwise there could be no principles of science or scientific laws. The mathematical forms of phenomena as well as their essential properties are derived from thought rather than through mere sense perception. Plato's dictum that facts cannot be scientifically ascertained devoid of thought introduced science to the world. This point of view was reinforced effectively by his contention that the forms or essence of data or phenomena could be mathematically expressed, that is, were subject to mathematical formulas.

Unlike perceptual phenomena that at best would produce a good and sometimes true opinion, principles of science would provide knowledge which is universally valid and which has an absolute quality. A person may accidentally arrive at a true opinion, but that does not mean that he is knowledgeable and expert. Perceptual data, argued Plato, "can never be the same as knowledge or science," because "knowledge does not consist in impressions of sense, but in reasoning about them."[16] Although phenomena might possibly vary from individual to individual, since each person has his own peculiar sensation of data (supplied to him by the senses), ultimate substance or reality must have its own essence independent of a person's perceptions. Furthermore, perceptions do not ascertain substantial or ontological reality, whereas thoughts, cognitions, understanding, and the cognitive processes do. While phenomena lack permanency, the ultimate substance-in-itself is eternal, for the ontologically real entities "have a permanent essence of their own."[17] Although phenomena (objects of sense perception) are relative to individuals who experience them, the basic realities upon which they are grounded must not be viewed as "fluctuating according to our fancy, but they are independent, and maintain to their own essence the relation prescribed by nature."[18]

What Plato sought to do was to distinguish and isolate true knowledge or scientific knowledge from mere or unsubstantiated opinion. Even a true opinion fails to qualify as knowledge, for it might be merely a lucky guess. Plato wanted a considered opinion based on scientific knowledge. A "true opinion, conjoined with definition, is knowledge."[19] That is to say, the Socratic criterion of truth involves a definition of reality; hence a definition of the real is what truth is. "Right opinion with rational definition or explanation is the most perfect form of knowledge . . . , for knowledge is not attained until, combined with true opinion, there is an enumeration of the elements out of which anything is composed."[20] When Plato spoke of knowledge and science, he meant what is known today as scientific knowledge, not technology (*techne*) which is only a craft or the skilled use of scientific instruments.

Anyone, for example, can look at a distorted tissue growth on a human body and report his sense perceptions of it, but only those with the proper scientific knowledge and understanding can report it as indicating a malignant disease. Plato objected to confusing everyday untutored experience with genuine scientific knowledge. Opinions, to be sure, often derive from one's varied experiences, and there are times when one can stumble on a correct opinion from personal perceptions, but a chance opinion that happens to be right does not qualify as scientific knowledge.

Knowledge, for Plato, was highly conceptual in character, comparable to the principles and formulas present in our contemporary science. Consider Einstein's classic formula: $E = mc^2$. Is this formula merely a thought, a theory without its corresponding entity in the real world existing outside of the human mind? If so, then it is merely a subjective thought devoid of any reality. If not, then Plato was right; knowledge has its counterpart outside of the human mind. In current philosophy, the so-called logical positivists deny that thoughts or principles are verifiable, that is, have an objective reference—a reality out there. In fact, the logical positivist, as an antimetaphysician, denies the existence of ultimate reality. Hence, a concept, such as electricity, does not exist inasmuch as it is imperceptible. Accordingly, logical positivists sympathize with the tradition of those early philosophers who believe in the existence of Heraclitian flux only or in the relativity of Protagoras; that is, they believe in the existence of phenomena solely because only the objects of sense perceptions are—in their estimation—verifiable. Because they repudiate any belief in ultimate reality and because they limit the domain of existence to the phenomenal world, logical positivists are labeled as phenomenalists.

In view of these deliberations, Plato is a realist rather than a phenomenalist, because he insists on the existence of an ontologically real world, a world of ideals. (The Platonic theory of Ideas will be discussed below.) It would be well to keep in mind that Plato's incorporeal world is the ground upon which science is constructed and from which scientific knowledge is derived, yet Plato's nonmaterial world of ideas must coexist with the corporeal world of phenomena. What makes Plato's philosophy most striking is the fact that he introduced nonmaterial or incorporeal reality into a system of philosophy. Plato's term for the nonmaterial was *asomaton*, that is, asomatic or nonsomatic, hence a bodiless reality or a world devoid of body—an incorporeal world.

III *Plato's Metaphysical Dualism: Appearance and Reality (Becoming and Being)*

Plato, accepting from Socrates the notion that conceptions correctly defined remain invariable, held that these conceptions must have their counterpart in the world of reality rather than in the world as perceived, that is, in the phenomenal world. On the other hand, objects of sense perception must have their corresponding object in the phenomenal world, that realm composed of Heraclitian flux. Aristotle, Plato's student, stated that Plato derived from Cratylus, a disciple of Heraclitus, the theory that the objects of sense perception undergo perpetual change. In his *Metaphysics*, Aristotle reported that Plato and his "supporters of the ideal theory were led to it because on the question about the truth of things they accepted the Heraclitian sayings which describe all sensible things as ever passing away, so that if knowledge or thought is to have an object, there must be some other and permanent entities, apart from those which are sensible; for there could be no knowledge of things which were in a state of flux."[21]

These permanent entities, the ultimate or ontological reality of which the universe is composed, Plato called Being (*ontōs*, from which we derive the word "ontology"). Plato's term *ontōs* is an adverb meaning "really," "actually," "truly," that is, the things that actually exist. To indicate this entity which Plato regarded as ultimate Being or final reality, he also employed the Greek word *ousia*, which means substance, being, essence, the true nature of an object, reality. Being or substance is ascertained through knowledge (*epistēmē*, from which philosophers derived the term "epistemology," the study of knowledge). The Greek word *epistēmē* connotes scientific knowledge, understanding, acquaintance with an object, "know-how" (skill), and science. From such knowledge a person becomes acquainted with the substance or essence of an object which is its reality; that is, one comes to know its inner Being or ontological nature.

Ultimate reality (Being) is beyond the reach of perception (*aisthēsis*). The Greek word *aisthēsis* denotes perception by the senses, that is, the sensation of a thing by sight, sound, touch, etc., or observation by the senses. Plato considered Being to be beyond the reach of sense perception; hence it must be ascertained through understanding. Although Being was not apperceived through the senses, Becoming (*genesis*) was. These objects (*genesis*) Democritus labeled *phenomena* as opposed to reality. The Greek term *genesis* signifies a created thing, something that had a beginning, a birth, that is, required generation and a process of aging. All objects of sense perception fall into Plato's category of Becoming (*genesis*). They represent the realm of appearance rather than the world of reality. Plato declared that "we participate in generation with the body, and through perception, but we participate with the soul through thought in true essence; and essence you would affirm to be always the same and immutable, whereas generation or becoming varies."[22]

In the *Phaedo*, Plato informs us that the etiology (that is, cause) of the phenomenal world of generation or perception is the Ideas solely, and that sense objects derive their qualities from the Ideas. He argues that there is "no way in which anything comes into existence except by participation in its own essence"[23] (that is, Idea or ideal reality). Note the sharp contrast Plato draws between appearance (generation) and reality (Idea). Genuine knowledge and understanding consist in distinguishing one from the other. In the *Republic*, Plato informs his readers that one only dreams when one confuses images for reality. A person's mind is truly awake when he discerns reality from appearance, true beauty from an object of beauty. "He who," inquires Plato, "having a sense of beautiful things has no sense of absolute beauty, or who, if another lead him to a knowledge of that beauty is unable to follow—of such an one I ask, Is he awake or in a dream only? Reflect: is not the dreamer, sleeping or waking, one who likens dissimilar things, who puts the copy in the place of the real object?" Plato continues: "But take the case of the other, who recognizes the existence of absolute beauty and is able to distinguish the idea from the objects which participate in the idea."[24]

For perceiving the phenomenal world (the realm of Becoming) and for scientifically knowing the ontologically real world (Being), human beings are equipped with two devices for ascertaining the twofold world with which they are confronted. By means of sense perceptions they apprehend the phenomenal world, and by means of scientific knowledge they comprehend the real world. From perception, Becoming is sensed; and from scientific knowledge, Being is cognized. Explaining these conclusions in the *Timaeus*, Plato wrote:

First, if I am not mistaken, we must determine, What is that which always is and has no becoming; and what is that which is always becoming and has never any being? That which is apprehended by reflection and reason always is, and is the same; that, on the other hand, which is conceived by opinion with the help of sensation and without reason, is in a process of becoming and perishing, but never really is.[25]

The world of Becoming (*genesis*) is in a continual process of becoming, but never perfects itself as fully Being. While it perpetually becomes, it never truly is, that is, it never attains reality. In his work, the *Sophist*, Plato viewed reality as Being and the phenomenal world as Not-Being. Not-Being must not be thought of as devoid of existence, but merely as lacking ontological reality comparable to a dream experience. That is to say, Not-Being is merely *other* than Being:

When we speak of not-being, we speak, I suppose, not of something opposed to being, but only different. . . . Seeing that the nature of the other has a real existence, the parts of this nature must equally be supposed to exist. . . . Then, as would appear, the opposition of a part of the other, and of a part of being, to one another, is, if I may venture to say so, as truly essence as being itself, and implies not the opposite of being, but only what is other than being. . . . Not-being has an assured existence, and a nature of its own.[26]

In discussing Being and Not-Being in his later writings, Plato did not have in mind the notion that Being exists while Not-Being is devoid of existence. Rather, he was citing two kinds of existence. The properties of a Being type of existence include perfection, universality, immutability, and the like, whereas Non-Being is characterized as being in perpetual process, becoming, developing, moving toward perfection though never achieving it. In the *Phaedo*, Plato informs us that "there are two sorts of existences, one seen, the other unseen." Regarding the former, "you can touch and see and perceive with the senses"; but as for the latter, "the unchanging things you can only perceive with the mind—they are invisible and are not seen."[27]

IV   *Plato's Theory of Ideas*

It is through the *dialectic* that *Ideas* (eternal and perfect reality) are ascertained, for sense perceptions cannot transcend the realm of phenomena to the region of ultimate reality. "And so with dialectic," asserted Plato in the *Republic*, "when a person starts on the discovery of the absolute by the light of reason only, and without any assistance of sense, and perseveres until by pure intelligence he arrives at the perception of the absolute good, he at last finds himself at the end of the intellectual world."[28] Plato's world of Ideas must be thought of as an ideal world: perfect, beautiful, immutable, eternal, and wanting nothing, for its Being is complete. By contrast, the world of phenomena is in a transient state, progressing toward perfection though never achieving it, imperfect, generated or created at some moment and in a given location, and its beauty is at best partial, with its development incomplete, for it is in a constant process of Becoming. More than merely being objects of knowledge, Platonic Ideas (Forms) are independently real of the particular physical objects of the world of perception in which they are embodied. Nevertheless, knowledge is derived from the world of perception.

The physical world of existence (Becoming) is a copy or replica of the eternal world of reality. By physical senses we make contact with the existent world that is restricted to the limitations of time and space. By understanding or knowledge, contact is made with the real world (Being) that is independent of space-time limitations.

Plato's Allegory of the Cave. What we have been calling the world of phenomena, Becoming, or the sense world is what most laymen would think of as the physical world or the material world. On the other hand, the world of ideas is comparable to the realities of science, such as, light waves, atomic energy, and other entities that transcend human sense perception and are ascertained by principles of science, that is, by the human mind through its application of logic, mathematics, and scientific method.

In order that his readers should appreciate the transition from the phenomenal world (physical world of Becoming) and one's ascent to ultimate reality (the ontologically real Ideas or world of Being), Plato offered an allegory of the cave. He asked readers to visualize some human beings imprisoned in an underground den. The den

has a mouth open towards the light and reaching all along the den; here they have been from their childhood, and have their legs and necks chained so that they cannot move, and can only see before them, being prevented by the chains from turning round their heads. Above and behind them a fire is blazing at a distance, and between the fire and the prisoners there is a raised way; and you will see . . . a low wall built along the way, like the screen which marionette players have in front of them, over which they show the puppets. . . . They see only their own shadows, or the shadows of one another, which the fire throws on the opposite wall of the cave.[29]

Although numerous people, carrying various objects, pass by the wall, only their shadows are perceptible to the inmates of the cave. Consequently, if the inmates hear an echo resounding from the other side, they cannot know definitely whether the voice belongs to a passerby or to a passing shadow. The inmates of the den would confuse a mere shadow for a genuine human being. "Truth would be literally nothing but the shadows of the images," observed Plato.

Even if these prisoners were released from their caves and told that the shadows were merely illusions, they, dazzled by the glare of the light, would persist in holding that the shadows are truer than the objects standing in the flesh. Only with time, as their eyes become accustomed to the light, would the prisoners appreciate the corporeal objects and become able to discriminate the superior reality of the physical object over the mere shadow of an object. "The entire allegory," wrote Plato,

you may now append . . . to the previous argument; the prison-house is the world of sight, the light of the fire is the sun, and you will not misapprehend me if you interpret the journey upwards to be the ascent of the soul into the intellectual world. . . . My opinion is that in the world of knowledge the idea of good appears last of all, and is seen only with an effort; and, when seen, is also inferred to be the universal author of all things beautiful and right, parent of light and of the lord of light in this visible world, and the immediate source of reason and truth in the intellectual; and that this is the power upon which he who would act rationally either in public or private life must have his eye fixed.[30]

Just as those prisoners dwelling in a den would prefer physical objects to shadows once they appreciated the distinction, so the persons who discover the world of ideals, of ontological reality, would prefer it to the phenomenal or transitory realm of existence. Plato would have us behold absolute justice instead of the mere shadow of justice, true beauty instead of the shadow of beauty, absolute truth instead of its mere shadow, and ideal goodness instead of just the shadow of goodness. That is to say, the nonsensuous ideal reality is superior to any object of sense perception, for a perfect thing invariably ranks higher than that which is in the process of striving for perfection and never can attain it.

The Character of the Platonic Idea. Considered by some authorities as the most celebrated term in philosophy, the Platonic Idea is a subsistent form or archetype, the nature of which is a transcendent universal. Although Plato employed the term "Idea" to denote a class name or species, he later, on reflection, identified its essence or truth as self-activity, the motivating principle in human nature as well as in vegetable and animal nature. It is the movement or motion responsible for all existence and change.

Having accepted from Socrates the conclusion that conceptions or essences, once accurately defined, are invariable and universally valid, Plato, regarding them as Ideas, concluded that their objective counterparts are to be found in a supersensuous world that transcends sense perception. These objects subsisting in that world lying beyond the scope of the senses to register, Plato termed Ideas or substance *(ousia)*.

Regarding the Idea as an archetype or paradigm *(paradeigma)*, Plato held that it was the universal form of particular physical objects of the sense world. Objects of sense "participate" or "imitate" the Idea, for they are merely shadows or copies of the universal Ideas or Forms *(morphai)*, as Plato occasionally referred to the ideas. Objects of sense perception, images, or phenomena are in a sense present *(parousia)* in Ideas, but Ideas exist (actually subsist) independently of them. Referring to phenomena, sense objects, and Becoming as Not-Being, Plato asserted that

the other [phenomenon] partakes of being, and by reason of this participation is, and yet is not that of which it partakes, but other, and being other than being, it is clearly a necessity that not-being should be. And again, being, through partaking of the other, becomes a class other than the remaining classes, and being other than all of them, is not each one of them, and is not all the rest, so that undoubtedly there are thousands upon thousands of cases in which being is not, and all other things, whether regarded individually or collectively, in many respects are, and in many respects are not.[31]

Ideas have the basic function of delineating the logical character of the common quality of objects of sense; that is, they are class concepts. Following Aristotle, modern philosophers and scientists refer to these common qualities as concepts. "Whenever a number of individuals [objects of perception] have a common name," wrote Plato, "we assume them to have also a corresponding idea of form."[32] Whereas sense objects are merely appearances, Ideas are ontologically real substances. While the Idea is the original prototype *(paradeigma)*, phenomena that are received through the senses are copies that imitate or mimic *(mimēsis)* the Ideal or Idea. "Copy is to the original as the sphere of opinion is to the sphere of knowledge."[33]

With the introduction of the Platonic Ideal, principles or concepts found their way into science and philosophy. There are some philosophers who hold that the world of Ideas of Plato is identical with the world of perceived objects (phenomena) which have been thought about conceptually. In this sense the Socratic concept as treated by Plato becomes an Ideal, a reality in its own right.

Definition of the Platonic Idea or Form. Let us conclude this discussion with a definition of Plato's conception of Idea. Plato's early dialogues favor an intensional view of the Forms or Ideas, referring to them in terms of shape, figure *(eidos)*, Form *(morphē)*, essence or substance *(ousia)*, Idea *(idea)*, and Pattern, model, plan, or prototype *(paradeigma)*. Concepts favoring an extensional viewpoint appeared in the later Platonic dialogues, in which the Platonic Ideas or Forms are referred to as unities, genera, or classes.

Notes and References

Chapter One

1. Alfred Zimmern, *The Greek Commonwealth: Politics and Economics in Fifth-Century Athens* (New York: Oxford University Press, 1961), pp. 67–68.

2. Aristotle, *Politics*. Translated by Benjamin Jowett (New York: Random House, 1941), 1252^a.

3. H. D. F. Kitto, *The Greeks* (Baltimore: Penguin Books, 1951), p. 135.

4. Aristotle, *Politics*, 1252^b–1253^a.

5. Plato, *Republic*, III, 387.

6. Plato, *Laws*, VI, 777.

7. Aristotle, *Politics*, 1271^b.

8. Plato, *Apology*, 24.

9. Ibid., 36.

10. Thucydides of Athens, 431 B.C., Book 2; see Arnold J. Toynbee, *Greek Civilization and Character* (New York: New American Library, 1953), pp. 38–39.

Chapter Two

1. John Herman Randall, *Plato: Dramatist of the Life of Reason* (New York: Columbia University Press, 1970), p. 10.

2. Ulrich Wilamowitz-Moellondorf, *Platon* (Berlin: Weidman, 2 vols., 1920), I, 42.

3. Aristotle, *Metaphysics*. Translated by W. D. Ross (New York: Random House, 1941), 987^a.

4. Diogenes Laertius, *Lives of Eminent Philosophers* (New York: Putnam, 1925), III, 6–7.

5. Eduard Zeller, *Plato and the Older Academy* (New York: Russell & Russell, 1962), p. 15.

6. W. K. C. Guthrie, *A History of Greek Philosophy* (Cambridge: Cambridge University Press, 1975), p. 19.

167

7. Paul Shorey, *What Plato Said* (Chicago: University of Chicago Press, 1933), p. 58.

Chapter Three

1. Plato, *Theaetetus*, 155.
2. Plato, *Phaedrus*, 250–52.
3. Plato, *Republic*, 485.
4. Plato, *Symposium*, 208.
5. Ibid., 204.
6. Ibid., 206.
7. Ibid., 206–207.
8. Ibid., 207.
9. Ibid., 211.
10. Ibid., 210.
11. Ibid., 211.
12. Ibid.
13. Ibid., 208.
14. Ibid.
15. Ibid.
16. Plato, *Phaedrus*, 238.
17. Plato, *Republic*, 581.
18. Ibid., 582.
19. Plato, *Timaeus*, 91.
20. Plato, *Republic*, 439.
21. Plato, *Phaedrus*, 237–38.
22. Plato, *Republic*, 583–84.
23. Ibid., 571.
24. Ibid., 571–72.
25. Ibid., 572.
26. Ibid., 605.
27. Ibid., 606.
28. Ibid.
29. Plato, *Phaedo*, 23.
30. Plato, *Republic*, 380–81.
31. Ibid., 381.
32. Plato, *Timaeus*, 70–71.

Chapter Four

1. Plato, *Republic*, 574–75.
2. Ibid.
3. Ibid., 575.
4. Ibid., 510.

5. Ibid., 511.
6. Ibid., 509.
7. Plato, *Theaetetus*, 176.
8. Plato, *Republic*, 444.
9. Ibid., 353–54.
10. Plato, *Philebus*, 66.
11. Ibid., 65.
12. Plato, *Cratylus*, 415.
13. Plato, *Meno*, 88.
14. Plato, *Philebus*, 23.
15. Plato, *Apology*, 37.
16. Ibid.
17. Plato, *Republic*, 428.
18. Plato, *Laws*, 689.
19. Plato, *Phaedo*, 69.
20. Plato, *Laches*, 199.
21. Plato, *Republic*, 429.
22. Ibid.
23. Ibid., 430.
24. Ibid., 442.
25. Plato, *Statesman*, 308.
26. Ibid., 306.
27. Ibid., 307.
28. Plato, *Republic*, 503.
29. Plato, *Laws*, 631.
30. Ibid., 633.
31. Ibid.
32. Plato, *Philebus*, 45.
33. Plato, *Charmides*, 159–65.
34. Plato, *Gorgias*, 494.
35. Ibid., 494–95.
36. Ibid., 506.
37. Ibid., 507.
38. Plato, *Republic*, 431–32.
39. Ibid., 430.
40. Ibid., 441–42.
41. Plato, *Laws*, 839.
42. Ibid., 636.
43. Ibid., 839.
44. Plato, *Gorgias*, 478.
45. Ibid., 508.
46. Plato, *Republic*, 331.
47. Ibid., 332.
48. Ibid., 353–54.

49. Ibid., 433.
50. Ibid., 444.

Chapter Five

1. Aristotle, *Politics*, 1271^b.
2. Plato, *Laws*, 628.
3. Ibid., 636.
4. Ibid., 836.
5. Aristotle, *Politics*, 1265^b.
6. Plato, *Laws*, 701.
7. Ibid.
8. Ibid., 742.
9. Plato, *Statesman*, 294.
10. Ibid.
11. Ibid.
12. Ibid., 301.
13. Plato, *Republic*, 558.
14. Ibid., 310–11.
15. Aristotle, *Politics*, 1313^a.
16. Ibid., 1253^a.
17. Ibid., 1263^b.
18. Ibid., 1269^b.
19. Plato, *Republic*, 358–59.
20. Ibid., 369.
21. Ibid., 433.
22. Ibid., 373.
23. Ibid., 416–17.
24. Ibid., 420.
25. Ibid., 465.
26. Ibid., 413–14.
27. Ibid., 414.
28. Ibid., 415.
29. Ibid., 473.
30. Ibid., 431.
31. Ibid.
32. Ibid.
33. Ibid., 432.
34. Ibid., 434.
35. Ibid., 457.
36. Ibid., 458.
37. Ibid., 456.
38. Ibid., 457.
39. Ibid., 551.
40. Ibid.

41. Ibid., 552.
42. Ibid., 555.
43. Ibid., 557.
44. Ibid., 557–58.
45. Ibid., 558.
46. Ibid.
47. Ibid., 560.
48. Ibid., 561.
49. Ibid., 567.
50. Ibid., 569.
51. Ibid., 563–64.

Chapter Six

1. Plato, *Republic*, 424.
2. Ibid., 388.
3. Ibid., 391.
4. Ibid., 402.
5. Ibid., 401.
6. Ibid., 403.
7. Ibid.
8. Ibid., 405.
9. Ibid., 411–12.
10. Plato, *Phaedo*, 73.
11. Plato, *Philebus*, 34.
12. Plato, *Meno*, 81–82.
13. Ibid., 84–85.

Chapter Seven

1. Plato, *Timaeus*, 48–49.
2. Plato, *Republic*, 500.
3. Plato, *Laws*, 741.
4. Plato, *Timaeus*, 47–48.
5. Ibid., 51–52.
6. Raphael Demos, *The Philosophy of Plato* (New York: Scribner's, 1939), p. 32.
7. Plato, *Timaeus*, 50–51.
8. Ibid., 50.
9. Ibid., 37–38.
10. Ibid., 38.
11. Plato, *Philebus*, 54.
12. Plato, *Timaeus*, 50.
13. Plato, *Parmenides*, 130–31.
14. Plato, *Phaedo*, 63–68.

15. Plato, *Republic*, 530.
16. Plato, *Timaeus*, 39.
17. Ibid., 41.
18. Plato, *Sophist*, 265.
19. Plato, *Timaeus*, 41.
20. Plato, *Republic*, 380.
21. Ibid., 381.

Chapter Eight

1. Plato, *Cratylus*, 390.
2. Plato, *Republic*, 532.
3. Ibid., 531.
4. Ibid., 510.
5. Ibid., 511.
6. Plato, *Theaetetus*, 152.
7. Plato, *Cratylus*, 356.
8. Plato, *Theaetetus*, 152.
9. Heraclitus, *The Fragments*, in *Source Book in Ancient Philosophy*, edited by Charles M. Bakewell (New York: Scribner's 1907), p. 33.
10. Ibid.
11. Plato, *Cratylus*, 402.
12. Ibid., 401.
13. Plato, *Theaetetus*, 160.
14. Ibid., 161.
15. Ibid., 171.
16. Ibid., 186.
17. Plato, *Cratylus*, 386.
18. Ibid.
19. Plato, *Theaetetus*, 202.
20. Ibid., 206–207.
21. Aristotle, *Metaphysics*, 1078^b.
22. Plato, *Sophist*, 248.
23. Plato, *Phaedo*, 101.
24. Plato, *Republic*, 476.
25. Plato, *Timaeus*, 27–28.
26. Plato, *Sophist*, 257–58.
27. Plato, *Phaedo*, 78–79.
28. Plato, *Republic*, 532.
29. Ibid., 514–15.
30. Ibid., 517.
31. Plato, *Sophist*, 259.
32. Plato, *Republic*, 596.
33. Ibid., 510.

Selected Bibliography

PRIMARY SOURCES

ADAM, JAMES. *The Republic of Plato.* 2nd ed. Cambridge: Cambridge University Press, 1965. Edited with critical notes, commentary, and appendices.

BAKEWELL, CHARLES M. *Plato: The Republic.* New York: Scribner's, 1928. Jowett's translation with introduction by Bakewell.

BLUCK, R. S. *Plato's Seventh and Eighth Letters.* Cambridge: Cambridge University Press, 1947. Edited with introduction and notes.

———. *Plato's Meno.* Cambridge: Cambridge University Press, 1961. Introduction, text, and commentary.

BURNET, J. *Plato's Euthyphro, Apology of Socrates and Crito.* Oxford: Oxford University Press, 1924. Edited with notes.

BURY, R. G. *Plato: Timaeus; Critias; Cleitophon; Menexenus; Epistles.* Cambridge; Mass.: Harvard University Press, 1942. Greek and English versions and introductions to each dialogue.

———. *Plato: Laws.* 2 vols. Cambridge, Mass. Harvard University Press, 1961. Greek and English versions with introduction.

CONFORD, FRANCIS MACDONALD. *Plato's Theory of Knowledge.* New York: Humanities Press, 1935. A translation and running commentary of Plato's *Theaetetus* and *Sophist.*

———. *Plato's Cosmology.* New York: Humanities Press, 1937. A translation and running commentary of Plato's *Timaeus.*

———. *Plato and Parmenides.* New York: Humanities Press, 1939. An introduction to and translation (with running commentary) of Plato's *Parmenides* and Parmenides' *Way of Truth.*

———. *The Republic of Plato.* New York: Oxford University Press, 1945. Introductions and notes.

DEMOS, RAPHAEL. *The Dialogues of Plato.* 2 vols. New York: Random House, 1937. Jowett's translation and marginal analysis, with introduction by Demos.

DODDS, E. R. *Plato: Gorgias.* Oxford: Oxford University Press, 1959. Introduction, text, and commentary.

173

FOWLER, HAROLD N. *Plato: The Statesman; Philebus.* Cambridge, Mass.: Harvard University Press, 1962. Greek and English versions plus an introduction by W. R. M. Lamb as well as his translation of *Ion.*

GRUBE, G. M. A. *Plato: The Republic.* Indianapolis: Hacket Publishing, 1974. Introductions to each book of the *Republic.*

——. *Plato's Meno.* Indianapolis: Hackett Publishing, 1976. This translation follows Burnet's Oxford text.

GUTHRIE, W. K. C. *Plato: Protagoras and Meno.* Baltimore: Penguin Books, 1956. Introduction with translation.

HACKFORTH, R. *Plato: Phaedo.* Cambridge: Cambridge University Press, 1955. Introduction, translation, and running commentary.

——. *Plato's Examination of Pleasure.* Cambridge: Cambridge University Press, 1958. A translation of Plato's *Philebus* together with an introduction and commentary.

HAMILTON, EDITH, and CAIRNS, HUNTINGTON. *The Collected Dialogues of Plato Including the Letters.* A collection of Plato's dialogues translated by a number of authors; each dialogue contains an introduction by the editors.

HAMILTON, WALTER. *Plato: The Symposium.* Baltimore: Penguin Books, 1951. Translation with an introduction.

——. *Plato: Gorgias.* Baltimore: Penguin Books, 1960. Translation with an introduction.

HARWARD, J. *The Platonic Epistles.* Cambridge: Cambridge University Press, 1932.

JOWETT, BENJAMIN. *The Republic of Plato.* 3rd ed. Oxford: Oxford University Press, Clarendon Press, 1888. Contains an introduction, analysis, and marginal analysis.

——. *The Dialogues of Plato.* 4 vols. New York: Charles Scribner's Sons, 1901. Translation with analyses and introductions.

——. *The Dialogues of Plato.* 2 vols. New York: Random House, 1937. Translation with marginal analysis by Jowett, with an introduction by Raphael Demos.

LAMB, W. R. M. *Plato: Ion.* Cambridge, Mass.: Harvard University Press, 1962. Greek and English versions with an introduction; also contains a translation by Fowler of Plato's *The Statesman* and *Philebus.*

——. *Plato: Lysis; Symposium; Gorgias.* Cambridge, Mass.: Harvard University Press, 1967. Greek and English versions with a general introduction.

——. *Plato: Charmides; Alcibiades I; Alcibiades II; Hipparchus; The Lovers; Theages; Minos; Epinomis.* Cambridge, Mass.: Harvard University Press, 1964. Greek and English versions with a general introduction.

LEE, H. D. P. *Plato: The Republic.* 2nd ed. Baltimore: Penguin Books, 1974. Translation with introduction.

LINDSAY, A. D. *The Republic of Plato*. London: Dent, 1935. Translation with an introduction.

————. *Plato: Five Dialogues*. London: Dent, 1938. *Ion; Symposium; Meno; Phaedo;* and *Phaedrus* translated by Percy Bysshe Shelley, Michael Joyce, Floyer Syndenham, Henry Cary, and J. Wright respectively, with an introduction by Lindsay.

RICHARDS, IVOR A. *Plato's Republic*. Cambridge: Cambridge University Press, 1966. Edited and translated into simplified English.

ROUSE, W. H. D. *Great Dialogues of Plato*. New York: New American Library, 1956. An inexpensive paperback edition translated by W. H. D. Rouse and edited by Eric H. Warmington and Philip G. Rouse.

SAUNDERS, T. J. *Plato: The Laws*. Baltimore: Penguin Books, 1970. Translation with introduction.

SHOREY, PAUL. *Plato: The Republic*. Cambridge, Mass.: Harvard University Press, 1937. Greek and English versions with an introduction.

SPRAGUE, R. K. *Plato: Euthydemus*. New York: Bobbs-Merrill, 1965. Translation with introduction and notes.

TREDENNICK, H. *Xenophon: Memories of Socrates and the Symposium*. Baltimore: Penguin Books, 1970. Translation with introduction.

VLASTOS, GREGORY. *Plato's Protagoras*. New York: Liberal Arts Press, 1956. Jowett's translation revised and edited by M. Ostwald, with an introduction by Vlastos.

SECONDARY SOURCES

ALLEN, R. E., ed., *Studies in Plato's Metaphysics* London: Routledge, 1965. Critical essays on Plato's theory of reality.

BARKER, ERNEST. *Greek Political Theory*. 1906. Reprint. New York: Barnes & Noble, 1960. Two fine chapters on Plato's political philosophy.

BARROW, ROBIN. *Plato, Utilitarianism and Education*. London: Routledge & Kegan Paul, 1975. A discussion of Plato's views on happiness, freedom, equality, and education.

BRUMBAUGH, ROBERT S. *Plato for the Modern Age*. New York: Crowell-Collier, 1962. Relates Plato's thinking to contemporary issues.

————, ed. *Plato Manuscripts: A New Index*. New Haven: Yale University Press, 1968. Index to the dialogues of Plato.

————, *Plato on the One*. New Haven: Yale University Press, 1961. Comments on the hypotheses in the *Parmenides*.

BRUMBAUGH, RENFORD, ed., *New Essays on Plato and Aristotle*. New York: Humanities Press, 1965. Critical essays treating Plato's degrees of reality, mathematics, and dialectic.

CORNFORD, FRANCIS MACDONALD. *Principium Sapientiae*. New York: Harper, 1965. The origins of Greek philosophical thought, with chapters devoted to Plato's philosophy, especially his doctrine of *anamnesis*.

CROMBIE, I. M. *An Examination of Plato's Doctrines.* New York: Humanities, 1963. A discussion of Plato's logic, methodology, metaphysics, cosmology, and theories of nature, forms, language, and knowledge.

CUSHMAN, R. E. *Therapeia: Plato's Conception of Philosophy.* Chapel Hill, N.C.: University of North Carolina Press, 1958. Platonic philosophy is regarded as psychotherapy.

DEMOS, RAPHAEL. *The Philosophy of Plato.* 1939. Reprint. New York: Octagon Books, 1966. A meticulous examination of Plato's views, without concern for what ancient thinkers (such as Aristotle) had to say about them.

FIELD, G. C. *Plato and His Contemporaries: A Study in Fourth-Century Life and Thought.* London: Methuen, 1930. Plato's life and work in the light of their moral, political, literary, and philosophical backgrounds.

FRAZER, JAMES GEORGE. *The Growth of Plato's Ideal Theory.* London: Macmillan, 1930. An analysis of the development and decline of the theory of ideals as it progressed in the mind of Plato.

FRIEDLÄNDER, PAUL. *Plato.* 3 vols. New York: Bollingen Foundation, 1958. Essays on various doctrines of Plato, including eidos, eros, and being, together with a comparison of Platonic theories with those of modern philosophers, such as Bergson, Schopenhauer, Heidegger, and Jaspers.

GOMPERZ, THEODOR. *Greek Thinkers.* 4 vols. London: John Murray, 1905. Volumes 2 and 3 are devoted to Plato's dialogues.

GOSLING, J. C. B. *Plato.* London: Routledge & Kegan Paul, 1973. A critical discussion of a number of Plato's theses.

GROSS, BARRY, ed. *The Great Thinkers on Plato.* New York: Putnam's, 1968. Discussions concerning Plato's philosophy by distinguished philosophers throughout history, including Aristotle, Augustine, Aquinas, Leibniz, Kant, Heidegger, Hegel, Emerson, Mill, Kierkegaard, Neitzsche, Russell, and others.

GRUBE, G. M. *Plato's Thought.* Boston: Beacon Press, 1958. Discusses eight topics pertinent to Plato's philosophy.

GUTHRIE, W. K. C. *The Greek Philosophers from Thales to Aristotle.* New York: Harper & Row, 1960. Two chapters are devoted to Plato's doctrine of ideas and ethical theories.

————. *A History of Greek Philosophy.* 4 vols. Cambridge: Cambridge University Press, 1975. Volume 4 treats Plato and and his dialogues exclusively, along with an extensive bibliography.

HARDY, W. G. *The Greek and Roman World.* Cambridge, Mass.: Schenkman Publishing, 1960. Excellent introduction for the beginner on fifth-century Athens.

JOSEPH, H. W. B. *Knowledge and the Good in Plato's Republic.* Oxford: Oxford University Press, 1948. Discusses Plato's epistemology and value theory.

KOYRÉ, ALEXANDRE. *Discovering Plato.* New York: Columbia University Press, 1945. An introduction to Plato's political philosophy together with translations of the *Meno, Protagoras,* and *Theaetetus.*

MORE, PAUL ELMER. *The Religion of Plato.* Princeton: Princeton University Press, 1921. The thesis is advanced that Western religious thought (Christian and pagan) develops in a straight line from Plato to the Council of Chalcedon in 451 A.D.

MUELLER, GUSTAV E. *What Plato Thinks.* La Salle, Il.: Open Court, 1937. Chapters devoted to Platonic love, the golden mean, polytheism, aesthetics, and Socrates.

_____. *Plato.* New York: Philosophical Library, 1965.

NETTLESHIP, RICHARD LEWIS. *The Theory of Education in the Republic of Plato.* New York: Teachers College Press, 1968. This edition contains a Foreword by Robert McClintock.

PATER, WALTER. *Plato and Platonism.* London: Macmillan, 1910. A series of lectures prepared for delivery to students.

PETTINGER, W. NORMAN. *Plato.* New York: Franklin Watts, 1971. Plato's life and teachings

PLOCHMANN, GEORGE K. *Plato.* New York: Dell, 1975.

POPPER, KARL R. *The Open Society and Its Enemies.* 2 vols. 5th ed. Princeton: Princeton University Press, 1966. The first volume, devoted entirely to Plato, develops some theories of Popper as well.

RANDALL, JOHN HERMAN, JR. *Plato: Dramatist of the Life of Reason.* New York: Columbia University Press, 1970. A personal account of the life and teachings of Plato.

RAVEN, J. E. *Plato's Thought in the Making.* Cambridge: Cambridge University Press, 1965. An examination of Plato's metaphysics in its process of development.

ROBINSON, C. E. *Hellas: A Short History of Ancient Greece.* Boston: Beacon Press, 1948. A discussion of Athens and Greece in the time of Plato, including a history of ancient Greece.

ROBINSON, RICHARD. *Plato's Earlier Dialectic.* 2nd. ed. Oxford: Oxford University Clarendon Press, 1962. An elaborate account of Plato's dialectic.

ROBINSON, T. M. *Plato's Psychology.* Toronto: Toronto University Press, 1970. Treated from the standpoint of rational psychology.

ROSTOVTZEFF, M. *Greece.* New York: Oxford University Press, 1963. This book consists of chapters from Rostovtzeff's *A History of the Ancient World.*

RYLE, GILBERT. *Plato's Progress.* Cambridge: Cambridge University Press, 1966. A criticism of Plato's dialectic is offered.

Ross, W. D. *Plato's Theory of Ideas.* Oxford: Oxford University Press, Clarendon Press, 1951. The gradual transcendence of Platonic Ideas is examined.

Sayre, K. M. *Plato's Analytic Method.* Chicago: University of Chicago Press, 1969. Intimates a likeness between Plato's philosophy and that of contemporary analytical philosophy.

Sesonske, Alexander, ed. *Plato's Republic: Interpretation and Criticism.* Belmont, Calif.: Wadsworth Publishing, 1966. A collection of essays by a dozen authors dealing with various aspects of Plato's *Republic.*

———, and Fleming, N., eds. *Plato's Meno.* Belmont, Calif.: Wadsworth Publishing, 1965. The *Meno* accompanied by a number of critical essays.

Shorey, Paul. *The Unity of Plato's Thought.* Chicago: University of Chicago Press, 1903. Emphasis on the coherence of Plato's philosophical ideas.

———. *What Plato Said.* Chicago: University of Chicago Press, 1933. Dialogue by dialogue exposition of Plato's philosophy.

Solmsen, Friedrich. *Plato's Theology.* Ithaca, N.Y.: Cornell University Press, 1942. Emphasis is on Plato's religious views as found in the tenth book of his *Laws.*

Stenzel, J. *Plato's Method of Dialectic.* Oxford: Oxford University Press, 1940. Discussion of Plato's epistemology.

Stockhammer, Morris, ed. *Plato Dictionary.* New York: Philosophical Library, 1963. Excerpts from Plato's dialogues on numerous topics.

Taylor, Alfred Edward. *Platonism and Its Influence.* Boston: Marshall Jones, 1924. Plato (as a theologian) is treated along with the Platonic tradition.

———. *Plato: The Man and His Work.* 7th. ed. London: Methuen, 1960. Although it was first published in 1926, it is still an influential introduction.

———. *The Mind of Plato.* Ann Arbor, Mich.: University of Michigan Press, 1960. Originally published in 1922 as *Plato.* It deals with the epistemology, cosmology, and psychology of Plato.

Voeglin, Eric. *Plato.* Baton Rouge: Louisiana State University Press, 1966.

Vlastos, Gregory, ed. *Plato: A Collection of Critical Essays.* 2 vols. Garden City, N.Y.: Doubleday, 1971. Technical essays on the metaphysics, epistemology, ethics, politics, and philosophy of art and religion of Plato.

———. *Platonic Studies.* Princeton: Princeton University Press, 1973. Essays on Plato for the advanced student.

———. *Plato's Universe.* Seattle: University of Washington Press, 1975.

White, Nicholas, P. *Plato on Knowledge and Reality.* Indianapolis: Hacket, 1976. Traces Plato's epistemology from the beginning to the end of his career.

WILD, JOHN. *Plato's Theory of Man: An Introduction to the Realistic Philosophy of Culture.* Cambridge, Mass.: Harvard University Press, 1946. Plato's philosophy is presented from the standpoint of a philosophical realist.

WOODBRIDGE, FREDERICK J. E. *The Son of Apollo: Themes of Plato.* Boston: Houghton Mifflin, 1929. One of the older influential books on Plato.

ZAKOPOULAS, A. *Plato on Man.* Translated by Sarah F. Alleyore and Alfred Goodwin New York: Philosophical Library, 1975.

ZELLER, EDUARD. *Plato and the Older Academy.* 1888. Reprint. New York: Russell & Russell, 1962. A reprint of an early classic.

ZIMMERN, ALFRED. *The Greek Commonwealth.* 5th ed. New York: Oxford University Press, 1931. A fine exposition of politics and economics during the time of Plato.

Index

180